MW00928624

THE MIND OF A GREAT LEADER

Become An Innovative Leader

MAHMIA R.

Copyright (C) 2024 by MAHMIA R.

All rights reserved solely by the author. No part of this book may be reproduced in any form without the permission of the author. The views expressed in this book are not necessarily those of the publisher alone.

First Edition 2024

Dedication

To my precious daughter Pranika,

At just two years old, you've already filled my world with wonder and inspiration. Your curious eyes and innocent smile remind me daily of life's purest joys. As you grow, I hope you'll understand that every word written here carries a father's learning and philosophy for making world a litter better.

With all my love,

Papa

Table of Contents

INTRODUCTION

Leadership is often perceived as a trait, skill, role, or a series of actions. Yet, at its core, leadership is an expression of the mind. How you think, how you perceive the world, and how you respond to the challenges you face will define your success as a leader. The mind of a leader is not just a tool; it is the framework where the future is envisioned, the present is navigated, and the past is carefully examined to drive progress, inspire others, and shape the future.

At the mind of a leader lies a distinct set of characteristics that distinguish them from their counterparts. They exhibit unwavering optimism, embracing challenges as opportunities for growth and transformation. They possess a keen sense of curiosity, demonstrate strategic foresight, willingness to challenge conventional wisdom, constantly seek new perspectives and innovative solutions, envision future possibilities and inspire others to join them on a journey towards a shared vision of success.

At the heart of a leader is a vision—a clear and compelling image of the future they wish to create. This vision pulls leaders through times of uncertainty and adversity by acting as a beacon of guidance and inspiration. It is the blueprint for change, the prism through which choices are made, and the impetus behind a leader's progress. It is more than just a list of objectives or aspirations. A strong vision provides the clarity needed to cut through the noise of everyday challenges, giving purpose to actions and direction to strategies. However, having a vision alone is not enough. The leader's mind must also be equipped with the capacity to think critically, empathize, adjust, or adapt in ways that allow them to connect the dots in unpredictable environments, make decisions under pressure, and empower others to reach their potential. In today's world, where the pace of change is rapid and the complexity of problems ever-increasing, the ability to pivot and redefine the course of action is a hallmark of great leadership.

Being a leader is a dynamic, ever-changing process of development, accountability, and service. The greatest leaders are those who are always looking to better themselves since leadership is a journey rather than a destination. They are aware that learning never ends and that they need to continuously update their knowledge and abilities. This dedication to development encompasses more than just learning new technical abilities or deepening one's knowledge in a particular area; it also entails honing one's leadership philosophies, challenging presumptions, and looking for fresh viewpoints. A true leader is never satisfied with the status quo. They are constantly evolving, not only to adapt to changing circumstances but also to challenge the systems, structures, and mindsets that may no longer serve their vision or the people they lead. The willingness to learn from others, to seek out feedback, and to embrace new ideas is essential to maintaining relevance and effectiveness in an ever-changing world.

Leadership is inherently about influence—shaping the thoughts, feelings, and actions of others in pursuit of a common purpose. The foundation of a leader's capacity to inspire is their sincerity and dedication to those under their direction. People who work with a leader who is motivated by a sense of purpose and leads with conviction are inspired. This is about bringing people's beliefs into line with the vision at hand, about being consistent and honest every day, and about proving through deeds what the goal means. It is not about using strong charisma or shallow appeal. People are inspired to not only follow but also to invest in the leader's vision as their own because of their genuineness and alignment, which also increases trust and loyalty.

Leadership is not without its challenges. The challenges of leadership are profound, and no leader is perfect. There will be moments of doubt, failure, and misstep. Yet it is in these moments that the mind of a leader is tested most intensely. Leadership requires the courage to face one's weaknesses, learn from mistakes, and persist in the face of difficulty. It requires a mind that is agile enough to adapt to new information, open enough to accept feedback, and strong enough to hold steady in moments of crisis. Above all, the mind of a leader, then, is not just a tool for strategic thinking; it is the very foundation of leadership itself—a reflection of character, purpose, and vision that guides one's long-term focus, even in the face of short-term obstacles.

Being a leader is a lived experience rather than a theoretical idea. The concepts covered in this book are intended to be used in practical settings rather than being abstract concepts. It serves as a template for not only those in leadership positions but also for anybody who wants to investigate the complex inner workings of a leader's mind and try to figure out what really motivates great leadership. The concepts we will discuss apply to everyone who wants to lead with impact, honesty, and purpose, whether they are team managers, employees, entrepreneurs, or top executives.

Chapter One

THE VISIONARY MINDSET

Vision is our perception of the future. Vision is a reflection of our goals and desires. It is our mental image of what could be but isn't yet. It offers us a sense of purpose in the future and still leads us through the present.

A visionary mindset is anything but fixed. Have you ever encountered someone who appears to be thinking ten, twenty, or even fifty years ahead? A visionary mentality entails the ability to look beyond the present moment, imagine a future state, and encourage others to engage in the pursuit of that goal. Leaders with this talent can see beyond the current issues and focus on the broader picture.

A visionary mindset goes beyond managing daily operations, in contrast to traditional leadership approaches that are only concerned with short-term growth. It lays the groundwork for long-term growth, innovation, and transformation, which makes it possible to create and recognize special connections and growth opportunities.

When it comes to leadership, visionaries are unique. They have the captivating power to uplift and encourage others, inspiring them to march in unison toward a common objective. Then, as they navigate the rough seas of uncertainty and challenges, their vision serves as a compass.

Understanding the Power of Vision in Leadership

The foundation of effective leadership is a compelling vision. It is a striking representation of a desired future rather than merely a declaration or an aimless wish. Leaders who possess the ability of vision can perceive, understand, and utilize things before others do. They do more than just spot the clear-cut opportunities, roadblocks, or signs of change; they also detect the subtle patterns and isolated incidents that only a vigilant eye can spot—things that seem unrelated and are frequently situated on the outskirts of our typical attention.

Great leaders are driven by the power of vision to break down barriers, bring people together, and pave the way for a better future. It offers a feeling of purpose, a clear direction, and a framework for developing plans, making choices, and carrying out actions. Great leaders use this power to shape the future and leave a lasting impact on the globe. Here are the powerful impacts of vision in leadership.

• Vision provides direction and clarity. Vision serves as a compass, guiding leaders through uncertainty. It provides clarity and guarantees that all efforts are focused on a shared objective. Leaders with excellent vision and direction abilities build settings or teams in which people know where they are going, and what is expected, and are encouraged to press forward despite any problems that may emerge.

• A visionary leader is unwavering in their leadership. A leader's strong vision facilitates decision-making by offering a framework for evaluating options. Leadership without vision can be quite frustrating and aimless.

• Vision encourages us to persevere. People are inspired and motivated by a compelling vision. It provides people with something to aspire to and believe in. A vision inspires, motivates, and provides focus and enthusiasm to individuals, groups and organizations beyond the non-discretionary and toward the discretionary. It concentrates and focuses effort so that daily responsibilities don't divert people, groups, or organizations from the bigger, more significant goals and purpose. A clear vision inspires individuals to be committed, tenacious, and eager to go above and beyond to give their 1000% all to achieve their goals. How big is your vision? As a leader, are you motivated to realize your vision?

• Vision fosters creativity and growth: Innovative leaders are frequently the driving forces behind innovation. They can think creatively, take chances, and create by seeing the future. Leaders who possess vision can question the existing quo and investigate novel prospects, propelling the development and advancement of both individuals and companies.

• Vision helps to overcome obstacles and thrive forward. The path to success will inevitably be fraught with difficulties and issues. You must know which way to travel when you encounter a wall or obstacle. You always have something to strive toward and look forward to when you have a vision. A clear vision serves as a reminder of the end result and the motivation for the efforts when difficulties emerge.

• Lasting influence. A visionary leader considers legacy and long-term influence in addition to short-term achievement. Their vision frequently transcends their own leadership, impacting subsequent generations and leaving a permanent mark on the world.

Essentially, visionary leadership is about recognizing what others do not yet see and motivating others to make it a reality. Serving as a lighthouse, a compelling vision unites efforts, energies, and resources while offering direction and purpose. It enables leaders to look past the difficulties of the present and envision an inspirational and attainable future.

Defining a Vision Vs. Having a Plan

Two fundamental concepts are frequently employed interchangeably in the context of success, leading to misunderstandings among experts, entrepreneurs, and laypeople alike. These concepts are planning and visioning. Planning and defining your vision are two different but closely linked concepts, both of which are essential to long-term success.

Let's begin by defining each of these terms separately to better comprehend them.

Defining Your Vision

A vision is a vivid and captivating mental picture of the future you want, frequently including your deepest goals, principles, and objectives.

A vision gives you focus, inspiration, and a feeling of purpose by reflecting on what you want to achieve or create.

Your vision serves as a compass for decisions and actions, providing answers to the "why" and "what" of your life or career.

Vision is comparable to the way architects see new structures and designs. Vision makes the purpose clear. The process of defining your vision entails painting an inspirational and unambiguous image of your future objectives.

Focus: The long-term, ideal future.

Purpose: The purpose of vision is to provide a future that pushes us to be more than we now are while still being reasonably achievable. It sets a standard, gives us direction, a line of sight, and the destination we hope to reach within a certain number of years. There are two ways to sum up a vision's purpose: to give our journey focus and clarity; and second, to make our lives and choices more in line with our core aspirations.

Examples:

- "To own the most streamed movie application in the world."

- "To create a world where everyone has access to clean water."

- "To become the CEO of one of the leading tech companies."

- "To become a beacon of hope and influence to generations by building a platform where everyone has the opportunity to share their stories and receive free counseling or therapy where needed."

Having a Plan

A plan is a defined path of action. It is a template for success. Simply said, it is the step-by-step process of defining how to attain a goal. It entails establishing clear goals, developing timetables, identifying resources, and determining the activities necessary. Plans are thorough, organized, and executable.

To connect us to our desired destination, planning entails determining in advance what to do, how to do it, when to do it, and who will do it.

Planning is ongoing and based on forecasts of future occurrences. It is a continuous process of adjusting to change. A fresh strategy must continually be developed in response to changing needs.

Focus: Short- and medium-term, actionable steps.

Purpose: To divide your vision into achievable activities and direct day-to-day decisions towards attaining it. Planning also aids in coordinating efforts at different levels. Without a strategy, an individual or organization will be tugged in many directions, causing confusion and misunderstanding at all levels. Planning is a tool for assessing performance. They contribute to directing conduct in the appropriate direction. They aid in avoiding errors, oversights, and deviations.

Examples:

- "Create an application for watching short videos next year."

- "Over the next two years, collaborate with three renewable energy firms."

- "Secure a job in a tech company by July."

- "This year, meet with 3 specialized trauma therapists and get their insight on how to create a community where people can feel heard."

Key differences between defining your vision and having a plan

- Vision comprises "what" and "why." It addresses the following questions: "What do I want to achieve?" and "Why do I want to achieve this?"

- Planning involves "how" and "when." It addresses the question, "How will I achieve this?" "What specific actions or steps are necessary?" In addition, "When do I want to achieve this?"

The relationship between defining your vision and having a plan

- Visioning is the act of identifying a new dream or goal, whereas planning is the set of procedures required to make it a reality. Without a vision, planning might feel aimless or unfocused. Without planning, vision stays a dream.

- Planning helps to make the idea a reality by establishing concrete tasks and schedules. Vision explains the "why" behind the plan's precise steps.

Crafting a Vision That Inspires and Mobilizes

Crafting a vision is painting a clear, appealing image of the future that directs choices, stimulates action, and offers a feeling of purpose. Here's a step-by-step guide to helping you craft a vision, whether for a personal goal, a business, or a team:

Self-Reflection: Start by considering your ideals, passions, and the times when you feel most fulfilled. Think about the legacy you want to leave and the influence you want to make on your business and others around you. To assist in the introspective process, ask yourself the following questions: What do I desire the most? What am I passionate about? What is my definition of success? What is my greatest dream in life and career? "How do I want to be remembered?"

- **Discover your purpose**

A strong vision is motivated by a feeling of purpose that extends beyond personal accomplishment. Finding your mission is a profoundly personal journey of discovering what motivates and makes you feel alive. It goes beyond professional goals or social accomplishments to include personal fulfillment and deliberate life. The Japanese notion of ikigai, which means "finding joy through purpose," elegantly describes the core of finding meaning. It captures the happiness and fulfillment we get from doing what we love. It occurs when what you enjoy, what you excel at, what the world requires, and what you can be compensated for all come together.

- **Define your core values**

Core values help us establish our limits and learn how to prioritize what is actually important to us, and they serve as a compass to steer us through life. While values might be generally stable across a lifetime, they may become more precise as we grow into our actual selves. Which ideals will govern your activities along the way? Is it about honesty, creativity, balance, sustainability, or empathy? These beliefs serve as the foundation for your vision and help ensure consistency in decision-making.

- **Paint a vivid picture of the future**

Leaders have an eye on the future. They can imagine the future. They can see more prospects by looking beyond the horizon of time. They can picture a bright future full of opportunities and excitement. After that, they might create a distinctive and ideal vision of the future and share it with others. Your vision must contain specific descriptions of the future, just like any good painting. When describing the future you see, use language that is emotive, clear, and detailed. When a vision is simple to visualize and connect with, it becomes more powerful.

For instance, "Imagine a society in which all children have access to quality education, a place where they are allowed to pursue their greatest potential and have huge dreams."

Our minds are strong instruments, and we should not undervalue the influence that our imagination may have on who we will be in the future. When you visualize the future you want, you construct mental images and new behavioral patterns. One of the most important steps in the success process is envisioning. It lets you see and feel what could result from the things you do today.

- **Create a life-planning routine**

A life plan serves as both a roadmap and a reminder of your goals in life. Additionally, a good template may assist you with everything from goal-setting to taking concrete measures to achieve those milestones, depending on how comprehensive you want to go.

You need a routine to help you organize your activities and evaluate your success if you want to continuously move toward your vision. Setting aside time on a daily, weekly, monthly, quarterly, and annual basis is ideal. Choosing what inspires and works for you is crucial, regardless of whether your life plan is a digital form like a Google Sheet or PowerPoint, something you print and complete, or even a bullet journal.

- **Highlight the Journey, not only the destination**

Life is made up of little moments. It's about mastering the ability to concentrate on and relish the success process. You miss out on all the wonderful things that happen along the road and may not even wind up be influencing anyone's life if you are only fixated on the end goal. An inspirational vision considers how the trip itself will transform individuals in addition to the destination. Don't rely just on your outcomes to gauge your achievement. Discover how to enjoy and concentrate on the success process. Honor the innumerable hours of work, effort, and time you devote to your goal. By doing this, you may accomplish your objectives more quickly.

Example of an Inspiring Vision:

"To create a future where every person, no matter their background, has the opportunity to live a life of purpose, dignity, and possibility."

This vision:

• Connects deeply with core human values (purpose, dignity, possibility).

• Is ambitious and bold, imagining a world of equal opportunity for all.

• Speaks to impact lives as it calls on everyone to make the change possible.

• Is simple, clear, and memorable.

The process of crafting a vision involves determining the fundamental ideals and concepts that direct your behavior, choices, and interactions with other people. These stages will help you create a vision that is in line with your beliefs and goals, as well as being clear and ambitious.

Setting SMART (Specific, Measurable, Achievable, Relevant, Timebound) Goals

The primary objective of setting SMART goals is to direct your time, resources, effort, and activities in a more efficient method. Put simply, it helps you avoid spending time on unrealistic or impractical goals. Goals are concrete actions that, if accomplished, directly contribute to your overall development. Establishing SMART goals enhances accountability and ensures timely progress, providing reassurance that you are successfully achieving your intended objectives. Here is a detailed discussion on how to set 'SMART' goals.

- Be Specific.

Life is a journey and unless you possess a clear destination in mind, you will persist in aimlessly meandering. A significant number of people wander aimlessly because of their lack of direction. To have any likelihood of achieving our goals, they must be formulated with precision and specificity. Establish specific goals. Don't just say "By 2025, I want to be independent." What are the things you'll do to ensure that you become independent? To be more specific, you can set goals like "Save $2,000 monthly for two years to start up my clothing business." Specific goals help you to assess progress and be encouraged to go further.

- Set Measurable Goals

In the SMART process, this particular stage requires you to use techniques for evaluating your advancement in attaining your goal. Evaluating your goals enables you to ascertain if you are advancing, helping you to remain focused and adhere to your planned timetable. When establishing a measurable goal, it is important to ensure that it is in line with specified metrics, such as achieving a predetermined amount of savings or obtaining a specific certification. The example I gave earlier, "Save $2,000 monthly for two years to start up my clothing business" is a measurable goal.

- Set Achievable Goals

Impractical and unachievable goals are not only vexing but can also squander valuable resources. To assess the feasibility of your goal, evaluate if it can be accomplished given the limitations of time, financial resources, skill level, external circumstances, and other restrictions that exist both internally and externally. When your goals are unattainable, it might be disheartening and discouraging. But by setting an achievable goal, you increase your chances of maintaining motivation and achieving success.

- Set Relevant Goals

Each goal you set should get you closer to actualizing your vision. It should propel you towards your core principles, aspirations, and future. Before setting your goals, consider the degree of relevance they possess. Check if your goal is significant to your life, how its attainment will benefit you, and its alignment with your overarching goal.

- Set a time frame for your Goals.

Efficient SMART goals should adhere to a certain time range. Setting a target date for achieving a goal enhances motivation and prioritization, while also instilling confidence by allowing you to monitor your progress. While not all individuals excel under time constraints, deadlines are crucial in guaranteeing consistent progress towards your ultimate objective.

Examples of leaders who transformed industries by focusing on vision

The effects of visionary leadership are felt by generations and sectors alike. Vision and purpose drive the most compelling leaders, and their vision influences each choice they make and action they take. They are their vision rather than just having one.

Steve Jobs

Co-founder of Apple Inc. Steve Jobs was a visionary leader who transformed several sectors, including digital publishing, phones, tablets, music, animated films, and personal computers. His unrelenting quest for innovation and excellence still has an impact on the IT sector.

Takeaway: Despite having a tough leadership style, he was always pushing the envelope of what was conceivable.

Reed Hastings

Netflix is a corporation that demonstrates how visionary leadership can guide a business through the rapidly evolving technical landscape. The company was founded in

1997 as a DVD rental service. The concept of purchasing DVDs online and having them delivered to your house was groundbreaking in and of itself, but Reed Hastings's ability to change course and become the world's top streaming service is a true example of visionary leadership.

Takeaway: Hastings not only had a creative vision and made it a reality, but he also managed to keep it afloat when the tides changed.

Shantanu Narayen

Many long-standing companies have failed as a result of the rapid developments in the computer industry. Shantanu Narayen, the CEO of Adobe Systems, decided to switch the company's distribution strategy from physical software to a digital subscription model after figuring out how the wind was blowing, so to speak.

Takeaway: Being a visionary leader involves more than simply coming up with novel concepts; it also entails being flexible and able to overcome challenges. Narayen is an excellent example of both of these traits.

In today's rapidly evolving landscape, the need for visionary leadership is more pronounced than ever. In a world fraught with complexities, uncertainty, and rapid change, leaders who can inspire and motivate through a clear, compelling vision are indispensable.

Chapter Two

THE ART OF STRATEGIC THINKING

O ne long-term method of addressing the underlying forces that shape life is through strategic thinking. Thinking strategically is being aware of what has not yet materialized, what may be approaching, and what may present a difficulty. The perspective shifts from "This is how things have always been" or "Why change what is not broken?" to "What can be done to change this outcome, please?" What can be done to expand this landscape?

Strategic thinking is required for making informed judgments and implementing action plans. It facilitates the analysis of several elements that may have an impact on the plan's success. Strategic thinkers are thoughtful and careful about their intentions to influence the future for both themselves and others, in addition to their decisions in the here and now. They are not only idealistic; they are visionaries with practical ideas who adapt to the shifting reality of their surroundings and foresee obstacles and changes in the market before they arise.

How Great Leaders Think Strategically About Decisions and Challenges

The value of strategic leadership is enormous. It helps leaders to view the broad picture, which includes brainstorming to stay ahead of possible issues and obstacles, build fail-safe procedures when necessary, and see opportunities to change course. Here are a few important ways leaders strategically handle decision-making and challenges:

- **Their vision and purpose are made clear.**

The first step for strategic leaders is to establish a clear vision and comprehend the organization's or team's overarching goal. Making sure that daily activities contribute to long-term goals, they match decisions and actions with the overall objectives.

- **They analyze context**

Context is crucial. It includes the who, what, where, when, and why of a circumstance or situation. It helps us to understand a problem from various perspectives. Contextual analysis is the process of deconstructing a complicated topic or issue to gain a deeper understanding of it. Contextualizing is a crucial component of decision-making since a poor choice could represent the difference between success and failure. Market trends, competitiveness, stakeholder demands, and organizational skills are just a few of the external and internal elements that great leaders consider before making choices. Strategic thinkers foresee obstacles and seize opportunities because they are aware of the environment in which they work.

- **They ask strategic questions**

While they may not have all the answers, great leaders ask the right questions. By posing thoughtful, strategic questions, they promote creativity and problem-solving skills and open up new avenues. It might be challenging to make decisions, but the process goes more smoothly if you ask the correct questions. Questions like "What is the growth trajectory for each of our services or products?" encourage leaders to carefully consider all of their choices before making a choice. "How should the organization respond to the emerging threat presented by the competitors?" is also an example of a strategic question that makes room for fruitful, solution-oriented conversations.

- **They are knowledgeable**

Leaders with strategic thinking skills are nearly always ready. They possess acute insight into the most pertinent market trends, identify chances to take advantage of and have a great understanding of what makes their firms vulnerable. They also tend to be flexible in response to new knowledge, even while they have goals for the future.

- **They are decisive**

The capacity to make prompt, well-informed decisions with the right amount of information is known as decisiveness. Time-sensitive and well-informed decision-making is essential. While weighing options is crucial before making a decision, some crucial choices cannot wait until all of the options have been considered. In light of the possible outcomes, great leaders look for and gather the essential information and determine when sufficient detail has been gathered.

- **They prioritize resources**

Time, money, and talent are all resources that effective leaders allocate to projects that will most effectively advance their strategic objectives. They concentrate on the most important areas that fit with their vision because they know that not every opportunity can be pursued at once.

Last but not least, strategic leaders are data-driven, forward-thinking, and capable of striking a balance between short-term goals and long-term objectives. They are proactive, flexible, and constantly aware of how internal and external factors are influencing the future.

Balancing Long-Term and Short-Term Strategies

In both the personal and professional domains, striking a balance between short-term and long-term strategies is essential because it lays the groundwork for long-term success. Even though instant gains and results might seem alluring, it's equally critical to think about how our choices and actions will affect things down the road. Ultimately, striking a balance between our short-term and long-term objectives has a big impact on our satisfaction and productivity in the pursuit of success.

Key differences between short-term and long-term goals

Establishing objectives is similar to creating a road map, but how long the journey takes is important. The following are some significant distinctions between short-term and long-term objectives:

• Strategic in nature, long-term goals set the course and ambitions for the future. More tactical in nature, short-term objectives concentrate on performance right away and support the individual's or organization's current overall success.

• While long-term goals span years, short-term goals are measured in weeks or months. The accomplishment of several short-term objectives is necessary for long-term strategies to move closer to the final vision.

You can better manage your objectives and make sure that your present and future needs are satisfied by being aware of these differences.

Management strategies to achieve the perfect balance

It takes a strategic mindset and the capacity to manage conflicting priorities to strike a balance between short-term and long-term thinking. Take into account the following important factors:

• Strategic Goal-Setting: Establish attainable short-term objectives that complement your long-term plan. Which short-term activities help me get closer to my long-term objectives? Additionally, set milestones to monitor progress and deconstruct long-term goals into manageable steps. Setting SMART goals was covered in the previous chapter.

- Time management: Long-term plans typically call for consistent work over an extended period. Short-term objectives can act as benchmarks or stepping stones. Make sure your weekly or daily activities support both short-term requirements and long-term advancement.

- Resource Allocation: A key component of implementing a strategy successfully is allocating resources precisely, which balances the requirement for immediate results with the pursuit of long-term goals. Think about the time, money, and effort you have available. It's crucial to pursue long-term goals (like changing careers or purchasing a home) without sacrificing short-term demands (like relationships or work performance). To avoid neglect or burnout, schedule time for both kinds of objectives.

- Iterative Method: Think about using an iterative strategy, in which quick fixes result in ongoing improvements. Because life is unpredictable, priorities might change. Staying focused on your long-term goals is important, but you should also be ready to modify your short-term plans of action in response to unexpected possibilities or difficulties.

- Measure and Evaluate: Create key performance indicators (KPIs) to gauge success and advancement over the long and short terms. Assess projects' efficacy regularly and make necessary strategy adjustments. If certain KPIs are easy to reach, try changing the metric to push yourself beyond your comfort zone and find the next big thing.

Analyzing and Mitigating Risk

Identifying your risks, comprehending how they may impact your success, and then determining what you can do to lessen their consequences are all necessary steps in risk analysis and mitigation. The procedure is broken down as follows:

Risk Identification

Risk identification is the first stage in the risk analysis process. Risk identification's function is to provide a list of possible hazards that can impair your capacity to accomplish your goals, reduce the adverse effects of threats, and increase your chances of success. To properly manage risks, it is critical to identify them early.

A few strategies to guarantee that every potential danger is recognized are as follows. Let's quickly review them:

• Self-assessment: Do you now possess any gaps in your skill set that might impede your ability to advance in your career? This might be dangerous, for instance, if you are not staying up to date with new technology or trends in the sector. Additionally, relying too much on one field of knowledge might present a risk if that skill becomes less valuable or obsolete over time.

- Sectioning: Risk identification can be quite difficult. Risk is complex. People, finances, the environment, and so on are just a few of the many categories. Divide your evaluation into each of these categories and examine each one separately. An overview study is a good place to start. What are the most obvious potential problems? Your everyday activities and company strategy may serve as the basis for this.

• Consult professionals: Talk about your plans with seasoned people, mentors, or colleagues. They could offer information about new dangers you hadn't thought of.

• Employ Risk Scenarios: To investigate the possible effects of various risk variables, such as internal problems (such as time restrictions or resource shortages) and external occurrences (such as natural catastrophes or economic downturns), create "what-if" scenarios.

Risk Assessment

A risk assessment is a methodical procedure that identifies possible risks and hazards in a scenario and then examines the consequences of those risks materializing. As a tool for decision-making, risk assessment seeks to identify which risks should be prioritized based on their effect and likelihood, as well as which actions should be taken to remove or mitigate those risks. The following are risk assessment methods:

- Evaluation of Qualitative Risk: Subjective judgment is used in qualitative risk analysis to assess the likelihood and consequences of a risk. It categorizes threats according to their probability (likely, unlikely) and severity (likely, medium, low).

- Quantitative Risk Assessment: This type of analysis uses numerical data or models to determine the likelihood and consequences of risks. It also makes use of past data from related occurrences or patterns. On a scale of 1 to 10, for instance, you can calculate that a company's computer system has a 40% risk of crashing during production. Hiring more employees to deal with these problems would cost $1,000 per hour.

- Risk Matrix: By presenting hazards in an understandable manner, the risk assessment matrix facilitates informed decision-making and is a helpful tool for communicating risk assessment.

Risk Mitigation

The process of lessening the effect of probable risks by creating a strategy to control, prevent, eradicate, or minimize setbacks is known as risk mitigation. To put it simply, risk mitigation refers to the strategies and methods used to reduce risk to a level that is acceptable. It uses tactics such as:

• **Risk avoidance:** When you use a risk avoidance technique, you take steps to prevent the danger from happening at all. For instance, ending a project with excessive uncertainty.

• **Risk reduction:** With this mitigation technique, you take steps to lessen the likelihood or effect of the risk once you've finished your risk analysis and recognized it. It acknowledges the risk and concentrates on limiting losses rather than eliminating them. Let's imagine you have a limited budget and there's a chance you won't have enough money to finish a certain job. By carefully controlling the expenses within the budget, you may lessen the possibility that that danger will materialize.

• **Risk transference:** Risk transfer involves passing the risk to a third party which is possible in the case of insurance companies.

• Risk acceptance: When the expense of risk mitigation exceeds the possible damage or when the risk cannot be avoided (residual risks), the risk is accepted. Although it doesn't have to be permanent, it can be the wisest course of action to accept some risks for a while. Occasionally, the reward may also exceed the danger.

Risk Review and Monitoring

Risk monitoring is responsible for checking if the degree of risk has changed since the last evaluation. Without keeping an eye out for the results and events that demonstrate the effectiveness of mitigation efforts, it is hard to put a response plan into action.

Adapting Pans in Response to Changing Circumstances

Change is unavoidable, and although some changes can improve your quality of life and be beneficial, others can be unpleasant and painful. Although it's normal to be resistant to change, there are a number of ways that making adjustments to your goals might benefit you and open up new possibilities.

Since change is unavoidable and continual, adaptability is necessary. It is the capacity to modify our ideas, actions, and goals to deal with novel, difficult, or complicated circumstances. Accepting change and modifying plans to fit new circumstances are crucial abilities in the fast-paced world of today. It's a crucial quality that helps people deal with life's ups and downs and react to unforeseen circumstances.

It takes time and concentration to learn how to be more flexible, and for most individuals, this process continues throughout their careers. You may increase your effectiveness in putting your ideas into action by effectively adapting to changing conditions and coming up with solutions for change. Gaining proficiency in this area might result in higher chances for personal development.

Exercises for Developing Strategic Planning Skills

These are the straightforward, tried-and-true strategic planning activities that are frequently utilized for creating objectives, determining priorities, and carrying them out:

• Set out at least two hours on your schedule beforehand. If at all possible, take a notepad, pen, and your preferred hot beverage to a lovely location. If nothing else, spend a few hours somewhere where you won't be disturbed or distracted.

• Make a self-evaluation by determining your values, weaknesses, and special talents and experiences (strengths).

• Jot down particular abilities or areas that you wish to improve (e.g., time management, leadership, and communication). Break down each area into actionable tasks or resources (e.g., books, seminars, workshops). Establish due dates for mastering each skill.

- Write a mission statement outlining how you plan to accomplish your vision, then a vision statement outlining where you want to be in five to ten years. Then divide your long-term vision into more manageable goals. Make sure every objective is SMART.

- Monitor results and make necessary strategy adjustments. Write down your accomplishments, difficulties, and lessons learned after each day or week. Consider how you can modify your objectives or tactics in light of these lessons.

- Set time priorities. Keep a record of your activities, including the amount of time you spend on work, hobbies, personal pursuits, and social interactions. Determine where time is being squandered or where it may be better used to achieve your goals for growth.

Chapter 3

CULTIVATING EMOTIONAL INTELLIGENCE

In today's dynamic and interconnected work environment, emotional intelligence (EI) has emerged as a cornerstone of effective leadership. Defined as the ability to recognize, understand, and manage our emotions and the emotions of others, EI plays a crucial role in enhancing interpersonal interactions and organizational outcomes. Pioneered by psychologist Daniel Goleman in the 1990s, the concept of EI has gained significant attention for its relevance in both personal and professional settings. Goleman explains that EI encompasses five key competencies: self-awareness, self-regulation, motivation, empathy, and social skills, all of which are essential for leaders who aim to inspire, support, and connect with their teams (Goleman, 1995). Research consistently supports the idea that leaders with high EI are more adept at fostering a positive work environment, promoting higher employee engagement, and navigating complex social dynamics within the workplace.

The importance of EI in leadership cannot be overstated. Studies have shown that emotionally intelligent leaders contribute to higher levels of job satisfaction and retention among their teams. For instance, a study conducted by Druskat and Wolff (2001) found that teams led by individuals with high EI demonstrated greater cooperation, creativity, and problem-solving capabilities. Leaders who are self-aware, empathetic, and skilled in managing their emotions create an environment of trust and mutual respect, which, in turn, increases employee loyalty. Furthermore, a meta-analysis published in *The Leadership Quarterly* indicates that leaders with high EI are 31% more likely to cultivate strong, positive relationships within their teams compared to those who lack these skills (Mayer, Roberts, & Barsade, 2008).

Therefore, this chapter explores the foundational elements of emotional intelligence in leadership, with a focus on three critical areas: self-awareness, empathy, and the ability to handle feedback and criticism constructively. Self-awareness enables leaders to understand their emotions, recognize their triggers, and assess the impact of their actions on others. Empathy allows leaders to connect deeply with their team members, fostering a sense of belonging and trust. Finally, the ability to handle criticism constructively is essential for personal and professional growth. By mastering these components, leaders not only enhance their own effectiveness but also create a supportive environment that fosters loyalty, respect, and long-term success.

This exploration into EI will reveal how these skills are pivotal in shaping resilient, engaged, and high-performing teams. With concrete examples, insights from scholarly research, and practical strategies, this chapter will provide a comprehensive guide to understanding and applying emotional intelligence in leadership.

Self-Awareness and Its Importance in Leadership

Self-awareness is the cornerstone of emotional intelligence and is particularly crucial for effective leadership. Defined as the capacity to understand one's emotions, strengths, weaknesses, values, and motivations, self-awareness allows leaders to evaluate their actions and recognize the impact of their behavior on others. According to Goleman (1995), self-awareness is foundational because it enables individuals to manage their own emotions and better navigate interpersonal relations. Leaders who possess a high degree of self-awareness can assess their emotional states, identify personal limitations, and leverage their strengths, allowing them to act decisively and authentically in high-stakes situations. This emotional insight facilitates decision-making processes, enhances communication, and fosters a transparent, inclusive environment, which is critical for team cohesion and trust.

Understanding Personal Emotions and Triggers

Self-aware leaders understand their own emotional responses and can identify their emotional triggers—specific situations, people, or feedback that elicit strong reactions. Emotional triggers often stem from deeply held values, past experiences, or internalized beliefs, and understanding these triggers can help leaders manage their responses more effectively. Research by Boyatzis and McKee (2005) in their work on *"resonant leadership"* emphasizes that self-aware leaders are better positioned to regulate their emotions, avoiding impulsive reactions that may negatively affect their teams. For instance, when leaders recognize that they feel frustrated during high-pressure situations or defensive when receiving critical feedback, they can work on strategies to pause, reflect, and respond in a constructive way.

Notable leaders have demonstrated the power of self-awareness by managing their emotional triggers thoughtfully. Consider Satya Nadella, CEO of Microsoft, who has openly shared how developing self-awareness transformed his approach to leadership. Nadella emphasized that understanding his personal biases and emotions helped him lead with empathy and flexibility, resulting in a cultural shift at Microsoft toward greater inclusivity and collaboration (Ignatius, 2015). Leaders like Nadella illustrate that by identifying and addressing emotional triggers, executives can foster a more supportive, growth-oriented environment for their teams.

Practical Tools to Build Self-Awareness

Building self-awareness is an ongoing process that requires deliberate practice. Here are some practical tools leaders can use to cultivate self-awareness:

1. **Mindfulness and Reflection**: Mindfulness is the practice of being present and aware of one's thoughts and emotions without judgment. Leaders can engage in mindfulness practices, such as meditation or reflective exercises, to enhance their awareness of emotional patterns. *Harvard Business Review* suggests that even a few minutes of daily mindfulness practice can reduce stress and increase emotional clarity, thereby promoting self-awareness (Brown, Ryan, & Creswell, 2007). Additionally, reflection—through activities like end-of-day journaling—helps leaders analyze their emotions and behaviors, identifying areas for growth and improvement.

2. **Emotional Check-Ins**: Another tool to increase self-awareness is the practice of emotional check-ins, where leaders periodically assess their emotional state

throughout the day. This could involve a simple exercise like "emotion naming," where leaders identify their emotions, such as frustration, anxiety, or excitement, and explore what might be causing these feelings. By naming emotions, leaders can detach from the intensity of the experience, gaining a more objective perspective. According to Siegel (2010), labeling emotions can decrease their intensity, allowing leaders to respond more rationally.

3. **Feedback from Others**: Seeking feedback from trusted colleagues and mentors can be invaluable for self-awareness. Sometimes, we are blind to our own behaviors and biases, and outside perspectives can help illuminate areas that require attention. For example, 360-degree feedback—a tool used by companies like Google and Deloitte—provides leaders with insights from peers, subordinates, and supervisors, fostering a holistic understanding of their impact (Gillespie, 2016).

Benefits of Self-Awareness in Leadership

The benefits of self-awareness for leaders are far-reaching, impacting everything from decision-making to interpersonal relationships. Self-aware leaders make better decisions because they recognize the potential influence of emotions and biases, allowing them to act with greater objectivity and rationality. For instance, leaders who are aware of their tendency to be overly cautious in decision-making might intentionally seek out data or perspectives that challenge their comfort zones, thereby fostering innovation.

Self-awareness also leads to stronger professional relationships. Leaders who understand their emotional triggers and manage their responses are better equipped to communicate authentically and handle conflicts constructively. For example, a leader who recognizes a pattern of defensiveness when receiving feedback may consciously adopt a more open and receptive posture, creating a safe space for constructive criticism. This self-aware approach not only improves individual interactions but also contributes to a culture of transparency and trust.

Companies that prioritize emotional intelligence in leadership often see tangible benefits in team dynamics and productivity. For instance, at Microsoft, Satya Nadella's focus on self-awareness and empathy has been credited with transforming the company's culture, fostering an environment that values collaboration, innovation, and continuous improvement. Similarly, Google's emphasis on leadership self-awareness through their "Search Inside Yourself" program has led to a culture where emotional intelligence is seen as integral to effective leadership (Tan, 2012). These companies highlight that when leaders cultivate self-awareness, they inspire similar behaviors within their teams, resulting in higher morale, engagement, and loyalty.

Building Empathy to Connect with Others

Empathy is a powerful component of emotional intelligence that enables leaders to connect meaningfully with others by understanding and sharing their emotions. In a leadership context, empathy means recognizing and valuing the feelings and experiences of team members, allowing leaders to respond in ways that foster a supportive and trusting work environment. Empathetic leadership helps bridge cultural, generational, and experiential divides, fostering a sense of belonging and psychological safety that is crucial for engagement and innovation.

Why Empathy Matters

Empathy is a critical asset for leaders because it facilitates genuine connections with team members, builds trust, and encourages open communication. When leaders demonstrate empathy, they show team members that their contributions are valued, which can significantly impact morale and engagement. Research from the *Center for Creative Leadership* (CCL) suggests that empathetic leaders are seen as better performers by their supervisors, as empathy enhances a leader's ability to resolve conflicts, support employee development, and inspire motivation (Boyatzis & Smith, 2006). Furthermore, a 2018 study published in the Journal of Business and Psychology found that employees who feel understood by their leaders exhibit higher levels of job satisfaction and organizational commitment (McKee, 2018). Empathy fosters a sense of mutual respect and loyalty, which are foundational for a positive workplace culture.

Empathy also allows leaders to appreciate diverse perspectives, a necessity in global organizations where team members may have different cultural backgrounds, work styles, and viewpoints. Leaders who are open to understanding these differences can create an inclusive environment where all voices are heard. This inclusivity not only strengthens the leader's relationship with individual team members but also enhances overall team dynamics. Google's **Project Aristotle,** a landmark study on team effectiveness, found that psychological safety, a concept closely related to empathy, is one of the strongest predictors of high-performing teams (Duhigg, 2016). When leaders foster empathy, they contribute to an environment where team members feel safe to share ideas, take risks, and support each other, all of which are essential for sustained innovation and growth.

Developing Empathy as a Leader

While some people may naturally exhibit empathy, it is a skill that can be developed through intentional practice. Here are key strategies that leaders can use to build and strengthen empathy within their teams.

- **Active Listening**

Active listening is one of the most effective ways for leaders to practice empathy. It involves fully focusing on the speaker, without interrupting, and responding thoughtfully to demonstrate understanding. Leaders can improve active listening by maintaining eye contact, nodding, and acknowledging what the speaker is saying. Brownell (2012), suggests that active listening not only helps in gathering important information but also demonstrates respect and empathy, as it conveys that the leader values the other person's perspective.

A practical approach to active listening is the "**three-second rule**," which encourages leaders to wait three seconds after a team member has finished speaking before responding. This short pause allows leaders to reflect on what has been said and formulate a thoughtful response, demonstrating that they are truly engaged. Leaders who practice active listening are better equipped to understand the concerns, motivations, and emotions of their team members, ultimately building stronger relationships and creating a supportive atmosphere.

- **Perspective-Taking**

Perspective-taking is the ability to scc situations from another person's point of view. By putting themselves in others' shoes, leaders can gain insights into their experiences, values, and motivations. Galinsky et al., (2008) found that perspective-taking is associated with reduced conflicts and improved relationships, as leaders who understand their team members' viewpoints are more likely to address their needs and concerns effectively

To develop this skill, leaders can engage in exercises like role-playing or scenario analysis, where they actively try to adopt the perspective of another person. For instance, in a challenging situation, a leader could imagine how a decision might affect a new employee, a team member from a different cultural background, or someone with contrasting career aspirations. Another way to encourage perspective-taking is to seek input from team members directly, asking them how they feel about specific projects or organizational changes. This proactive approach not only provides leaders with valuable insights but also makes team members feel respected and valued.

The Impact of Empathy on Teams

Empathy in leadership has a transformative effect on team dynamics, morale, and loyalty. Teams led by empathetic leaders tend to have higher levels of trust and cooperation, which lead to stronger performance and engagement. One notable example is Starbucks, whose former CEO, Howard Schultz, emphasized empathy as a central tenet of the company's culture. Schultz believed that understanding the needs and feelings of employees was key to creating a sense of belonging. Under his leadership, Starbucks implemented policies that focused on employee well-being, including health benefits and education assistance for part-time employees. Schultz's empathetic approach led to high levels of employee satisfaction and loyalty, which contributed to Starbucks' reputation as an employer of choice and its continued success as a global brand (Schultz & Gordon, 2011).

Another example is **Google's Project Oxygen**, which identified empathy as a key characteristic of their best managers. The study revealed that managers who practiced empathy by listening to their teams, supporting their growth, and showing personal interest in their well-being had the most positive impact on team performance. These managers created a work environment that encouraged creativity and open dialogue, ultimately enhancing the company's innovative capabilities (Garvin, 2013). Through this research, Google recognized that empathy is not only a "soft skill" but a critical driver of operational success.

Empathy also plays a significant role in retaining talent. A 2019 survey by Businessolver found that 93% of employees would stay with an empathetic employer, highlighting that leaders who practice empathy have an advantage in reducing turnover. In today's competitive talent landscape, where retaining skilled employees is a priority for many organizations, empathy serves as a key differentiator that attracts and keeps top talent (Businessolver, 2019). By building connections, understanding individual challenges, and addressing concerns empathetically, leaders can cultivate a loyal and engaged workforce.

Handling Feedback and Criticism Constructively

Handling feedback and criticism is a crucial skill for leaders, as it directly impacts their growth and the atmosphere of their teams. While feedback can be essential for improvement, it often triggers defensive or emotional responses, making it challenging to manage constructively. Emotional intelligence (EI) plays a vital role in helping leaders respond to criticism thoughtfully, rather than impulsively. Leaders with high EI can separate emotion from feedback, view criticism as a tool for growth, and ultimately use it to strengthen both their leadership abilities and team relationships.

The Role of EI in Handling Feedback

Receiving feedback can be difficult because it often challenges one's self-perception, which can lead to defensive reactions. Leaders with strong EI recognize that emotional responses to criticism—such as frustration or defensiveness—are natural but can be controlled to avoid negative outcomes. Research from the *Journal of Organizational Behavior* suggests that emotionally intelligent leaders are more likely to welcome feedback, as they view it as an opportunity to learn rather than a personal affront (Caruso, Mayer, & Salovey, 2002). This mindset allows them to remain open to feedback, thereby encouraging a culture of continuous improvement within their teams.

Leaders who manage feedback constructively set a positive example for their teams, demonstrating that mistakes or areas for improvement are part of the growth process. This approach creates a supportive environment where team members feel safe sharing ideas and taking risks, knowing that feedback is a tool for growth rather than punishment. Research by Druskat and Wolff (2001) shows that teams with emotionally intelligent leaders report higher levels of psychological safety, which is crucial for collaboration, innovation, and overall performance.

Techniques for Constructive Feedback Management

To handle feedback and criticism constructively, leaders can apply specific EI-based techniques that allow them to process feedback thoughtfully and use it as a tool for improvement.

- **Separating Emotion from Feedback**

A key technique in managing feedback constructively is to separate emotion from the information being received. Leaders who immediately react to criticism often do so emotionally, which can lead to impulsive responses that may harm relationships and reduce the effectiveness of the feedback. Instead, emotionally intelligent leaders practice pausing before responding, allowing them time to process the information rationally.

One strategy is to adopt a 24-hour rule: when receiving feedback, leaders can acknowledge it and express their intent to consider it, then take time to reflect before responding. This cooling-off period helps reduce the emotional impact, allowing leaders to analyze the feedback more objectively. By pausing, leaders can identify whether their emotional response stems from ego, insecurity, or genuine disagreement, which in turn informs a more thoughtful response. According to Schilling (2009), that delaying responses to criticism can lead to more constructive outcomes, as it allows leaders to respond from a place of composure rather than reaction.

- **Focusing on Growth**

Another effective approach is to adopt a growth mindset, which reframes criticism as an opportunity for self-improvement. Carol Dweck (2006), a psychologist known for her work on mindset, suggests that individuals who see challenges as learning opportunities are more resilient and open to feedback. Leaders with a growth mindset use criticism as a way to identify skill gaps and make necessary adjustments, viewing feedback as beneficial rather than threatening.

By focusing on growth, leaders can actively seek out feedback to address areas of development, signaling to their teams that they are committed to self-improvement. For instance, leaders can ask follow-up questions to gain a deeper understanding of specific feedback, which demonstrates a proactive attitude and a genuine interest in learning. This approach not only enhances the leader's own performance but also creates a team culture where feedback is viewed positively and individuals feel encouraged to seek constructive criticism for their own development.

Using EI to Provide Feedback Effectively

Emotionally intelligent leaders are skilled not only at receiving feedback but also at providing it in a constructive, non-threatening way. Effective feedback requires sensitivity and consideration of the recipient's emotions, as well as the ability to communicate in a manner that motivates improvement rather than discouragement. A study from the **Academy of Management** reveals that feedback is most effective when delivered with empathy and a focus on actionable insights (Ashford & Cummings, 1983).

Emotionally intelligent leaders provide feedback in a way that highlights areas for improvement without attacking the individual. One effective method is the "situation-behavior-impact" (SBI) model, where leaders describe the situation, focus on specific behaviors, and explain the impact of those behaviors on the team or project. For example, instead of saying, "Your work was sloppy," a leader could say, "In yesterday's report (situation), I noticed there were some data discrepancies (behavior), which made it challenging to analyze the findings accurately (impact). Let's work together to prevent this in future reports." This approach keeps the feedback specific and objective, which reduces defensiveness and focuses on constructive solutions.

Practical Scenarios

Constructive feedback and effective responses to criticism can transform potential setbacks into growth opportunities. One well-known example is the case of Ed Catmull, co-founder of Pixar Animation Studios. Catmull cultivated an open feedback culture at Pixar by creating "Braintrust" meetings, where directors and creative teams gave and received candid feedback on movie projects. Catmull's emphasis on constructive feedback—focused on improvement rather than blame—allowed Pixar's teams to embrace criticism as a way to enhance creativity and storytelling (Catmull & Wallace, 2014). This approach contributed to Pixar's sustained success, as teams continuously refined their work in response to constructive insights.

Another example comes from Microsoft under the leadership of Satya Nadella. Upon becoming CEO, Nadella promoted a growth mindset within the company, emphasizing that feedback and failure are essential parts of innovation. His approach led to significant cultural shifts, with employees feeling empowered to experiment, share constructive feedback, and learn from mistakes. Nadella's focus on using feedback constructively has been widely credited with Microsoft's resurgence in recent years, as the company became known for fostering a collaborative and supportive work culture (Ignatius, 2015).

On an individual level, leaders can apply these principles in everyday interactions with their teams. For instance, a manager receiving feedback about being overly directive might take time to reflect on whether their behavior could indeed limit team members' autonomy. Rather than dismissing the criticism, the manager could commit to gradually giving more decision-making authority to the team, viewing the feedback as an opportunity to enhance team dynamics.

How Emotional Intelligence Fosters Loyalty and Respect

Emotional intelligence (EI) has proven to be a foundational element in fostering loyalty and respect within organizations. Leaders who demonstrate high EI can understand and manage their own emotions, empathize with others, and communicate effectively, which creates a work environment where employees feel valued and motivated. Research consistently links EI with greater employee loyalty, lower turnover rates, and a high level of respect for leaders.

Creating a Loyal Workforce

Loyalty in the workforce arises when employees feel valued, respected, and supported in their roles. Leaders with strong EI foster an environment that fulfills these needs by prioritizing open communication, recognizing employee contributions, and showing genuine concern for their teams' well-being. Research shows that when leaders actively practice empathy and mindfulness, they create a culture where employees feel safe, appreciated, and more committed to the organization. A study by Gallup found that organizations with empathetic, emotionally intelligent leaders have 21% higher profitability and 41% lower absenteeism, as employees in these environments tend to show greater dedication and are less likely to seek employment elsewhere (Gallup, 2020).

Furthermore, emotionally intelligent leaders encourage continuous growth and development, fostering a culture that not only attracts talent but retains it. They understand that fostering loyalty involves recognizing each employee's unique strengths, offering constructive feedback, and providing opportunities for advancement. This approach empowers employees, boosting their confidence and encouraging a sense of belonging. In workplaces where EI is emphasized, employees are more likely to report feelings of pride in their work and a personal connection to the organization's mission, leading to long-term loyalty.

In conclusion, emotional intelligence (EI) is a transformative skill that underpins effective leadership. Leaders who cultivate self-awareness, empathy, and the ability to handle feedback constructively are better equipped to inspire loyalty, foster trust, and maintain positive team dynamics. Self-awareness enables leaders to understand their emotions and their impact, while empathy helps them connect deeply with others, creating an inclusive, supportive environment. By handling criticism with openness and a growth mindset, emotionally intelligent leaders demonstrate resilience and set a constructive tone for their teams. Together, these aspects of EI contribute to a workplace where employees feel valued, respected, and motivated.

As the demands of modern leadership continue to evolve, EI remains essential for those aiming to build strong, cohesive teams. Leaders with high emotional intelligence not only enhance their own effectiveness but also create work environments that prioritize well-being and collaboration, leading to higher employee engagement and reduced turnover. The success stories of leaders like Satya Nadella and Howard Schultz illustrate how incorporating EI into leadership practices can transform organizational culture and drive sustained growth.

To those aspiring to strengthen their leadership skills, now is the time to embrace and develop your emotional intelligence. Practice self-reflection, listen actively, and approach feedback as an opportunity for growth. By doing so, you will not only become a better leader but will also empower your team to reach new heights.

Chapter Four

BUILDING RESILIENCE AND MENTAL TOUGHNESS

In today's complex world, resilience and mental toughness are indispensable traits for effective leadership. Both qualities allow leaders to withstand setbacks, maintain focus in challenging situations, and inspire confidence in their teams. Resilience is the ability to bounce back from adversity, adapt to changes, and keep moving forward despite obstacles. Mental toughness, closely related to resilience, encompasses the inner strength, determination, and persistence that leaders need to stay committed to their goals in the face of stress, failure, and unpredictability. Together, resilience and mental toughness create a foundation for leaders to handle the challenges of a fast-paced and uncertain world with poise and clarity.

The need for resilient leaders is especially pronounced in today's environment, where constant change and disruption are the norms. Rapid technological advances, global competition, economic instability, and unforeseen events, like the COVID-19 pandemic, have highlighted the importance of leaders who can navigate through uncertainty and help their teams do the same. In this context, resilience becomes not only a personal asset but also a critical factor in organizational stability and growth. Leaders with mental toughness possess the mental agility to pivot strategies, manage emotions, and maintain optimism, enabling their teams to remain productive and focused amid challenging circumstances. Resilience, therefore, is more than an individual trait—it is a driving force that contributes to an organization's overall success.

This chapter will explore the critical components of resilience and mental toughness, beginning with the development of perseverance and grit. Perseverance, or sustained effort over time, paired with grit—a blend of passion and persistence for long-term goals—enables leaders to remain steadfast in the pursuit of their vision, even when faced with repeated setbacks. Additionally, we will examine the role of failure as a powerful learning opportunity. While failure can be disheartening, resilient leaders see it as a chance to gain insights, improve strategies, and refine their approach. By reframing setbacks as stepping stones, they strengthen their adaptability and capacity for innovation.

Finally, this chapter will provide practical techniques for maintaining mental resilience. Building resilience is an ongoing process that involves nurturing mental, emotional, and physical well-being. Techniques such as mindfulness, physical fitness, and cultivating supportive relationships help leaders manage stress and enhance their capacity to cope with pressure. By integrating these practices, leaders can develop a resilient mindset that allows them to remain composed, strategic, and focused, even when facing significant adversity.

In addition to exploring these themes, we will delve into case studies of notable leaders who have demonstrated resilience in the face of hardship. Their experiences serve as powerful examples of how resilience and mental toughness can be harnessed to overcome obstacles and achieve remarkable success. Through these case studies and actionable insights, this chapter aims to equip readers with the knowledge and tools to build their resilience, empowering them to thrive as leaders regardless of the challenges they face.

This journey through resilience will highlight how perseverance, the ability to embrace failure, and the practice of mental resilience techniques form the foundation of effective, enduring leadership. As leaders build these qualities, they become better equipped to navigate today's demanding environment, serve as sources of strength for their teams, and ultimately drive their organizations toward success in an ever-changing world.

The Role of Resilience in Overcoming Setbacks and Leading Through Tough Times

Resilience is the ability to adapt, recover, and grow stronger in the face of adversity. In a leadership context, resilience goes beyond simply enduring tough situations; it involves a proactive approach to challenges, finding ways to move forward, and remaining committed to long-term goals despite setbacks. Psychological research defines resilience as the mental and emotional flexibility that enables individuals to adjust to difficult circumstances and continue working effectively. Leaders who embody resilience can manage stress, inspire those around them, and provide a steadying influence, helping their teams persevere through uncertainty and come out stronger on the other side.

Historically, resilience has been identified as a defining quality of influential leaders. Studies in psychology and organizational behavior suggest that resilient leaders not only adapt to challenges themselves but also create environments that foster resilience within their teams. For example, Dr. Martin Seligman's research on positive psychology highlights that resilient individuals tend to have an optimistic yet realistic outlook. This mindset enables leaders to see opportunities within challenges and communicate this perspective to their teams, fostering a culture of resilience that reinforces organizational strength. In times of crisis, resilient leaders are able to confront reality, accept ambiguity, and focus on actionable solutions, helping to instill confidence and stability across the organization.

Why Leaders Need Resilience

Resilience is essential for leaders, especially in difficult times, because it provides them with the mental and emotional tools needed to navigate complex challenges. Leaders who are resilient can effectively manage stress, maintain composure, and provide direction even when the future is uncertain. This capacity to remain calm and grounded under pressure is essential not only for the leader's own well-being but also for maintaining team morale. When a leader demonstrates resilience, they set an example for their team, encouraging them to stay focused, adaptable, and engaged despite obstacles.

Furthermore, resilient leaders can inspire confidence, offering reassurance to those who may feel uncertain or discouraged. By projecting a sense of hope and possibility, these leaders help their teams stay motivated, making it easier for them to work through challenges together. Resilience also supports decision-making by helping leaders remain clear-headed and rational, avoiding impulsive choices that could worsen a situation. In times of upheaval, leaders who demonstrate resilience are able to build trust, foster loyalty, and create a shared sense of purpose, guiding their teams through hardship while maintaining organizational cohesion and morale.

Real-World Examples

Numerous companies and leaders have faced adversity and emerged stronger due to resilience. For instance, after the September 11 attacks in 2001, New York-based companies faced enormous financial and operational challenges. Howard Lutnick, CEO of Cantor Fitzgerald, lost a significant portion of his workforce in the attacks. Despite immense personal and organizational loss, Lutnick led the firm through one of its darkest periods, rebuilding the business and implementing long-term support for the families of lost employees. His resilience, as well as his willingness to take responsibility and care for those impacted, helped Cantor Fitzgerald recover and eventually thrive again.

Similarly, the 2008 financial crisis saw several industries in disarray, with financial institutions particularly affected. JPMorgan Chase CEO Jamie Dimon exemplified resilience, navigating the bank through the crisis with strategic, steady leadership. Dimon's approach involved open communication, transparency, and calculated decision-making, all while maintaining a focus on long-term sustainability rather than short-term profit. This resilience not only helped the bank survive the crisis but also positioned it as one of the most stable financial institutions in the years that followed.

More recently, during the COVID-19 pandemic, many leaders faced unprecedented challenges. Arne Sorenson, the late CEO of Marriott International, demonstrated resilience by openly communicating the impact of the pandemic on the hospitality industry. Sorenson's heartfelt communication and empathetic leadership helped employees feel connected and supported, even as the company faced substantial layoffs. By acknowledging the hardships and expressing his commitment to the company's future, Sorenson provided a model of resilient leadership that inspired confidence and loyalty during an uncertain time.

Practical Insights for Building Resilience as a Leader

Resilient leaders exhibit several key behaviors that allow them to persevere through challenging times. These include:

1. **Adaptive Thinking**: Resilient leaders maintain a flexible mindset, adjusting strategies as needed and remaining open to change. This adaptability allows them to

respond constructively to unforeseen obstacles, viewing them as opportunities to innovate and grow.

2. **Emotional Regulation**: Leaders with resilience are able to manage their emotions, maintaining calmness and clarity even under intense stress. This emotional control helps them make rational decisions and prevents negative emotions from influencing their actions or communication.

3. **Effective Communication**: Resilient leaders prioritize transparent, empathetic communication. They keep their teams informed about challenges and potential solutions, fostering trust and unity by showing respect and understanding for the team's experiences.

4. **Optimism Balanced with Realism**: Resilient leaders find a balance between optimism and realism, acknowledging challenges while focusing on positive outcomes. This dual focus helps them inspire hope without downplaying the reality of difficult situations.

5. **Focus on Growth and Learning**: Instead of viewing setbacks as failures, resilient leaders treat them as learning opportunities. They reflect on what went wrong, identify areas for improvement, and apply these insights to future situations.

Developing Perseverance and Grit

Perseverance and grit are two traits that contribute to

resilience by fueling the drive to overcome obstacles and maintain momentum toward long-term goals. Though often used interchangeably, they each have distinct characteristics. Perseverance refers to the sustained effort to push through challenges and remain consistent in the face of difficulty. Grit, as defined by psychologist Angela Duckworth, is the combination of passion and sustained effort directed toward long-term goals. Together, perseverance and grit create a powerful force that enables individuals to endure and excel, especially when faced with adversity.

Angela Duckworth's research on grit has brought the concept into popular discussions on success and resilience. Her studies reveal that grit—more than intelligence, talent, or socioeconomic background—often predicts high levels of achievement. In her work, Duckworth found that people who demonstrate high levels of grit tend to outperform those with higher IQ scores in challenging fields like the military, academia, and competitive business environments. The research suggests that, while talent and intelligence are valuable, the relentless pursuit of goals over time can play a more decisive role in one's success.

Building Perseverance and Grit

Here are some actionable ways to cultivate perseverance and grit:

1. **Set Ambitious Yet Achievable Goals**: Start by setting

goals that stretch your abilities but are attainable with effort and persistence. Break down larger objectives into smaller, manageable steps. By accomplishing each step, you build a sense of progress and build resilience against the frustration that comes from daunting, unstructured goals.

2. **Learn from Minor Setbacks**: Setbacks are inevitable, but they also present valuable learning opportunities. Viewing failures as feedback can build perseverance. By analyzing what went wrong and adjusting your approach, you develop the mental flexibility and determination needed to continue moving forward, even in the face of challenges.

3. **Stay Committed to the Larger Vision**: Leaders with grit often keep a clear view of their overarching vision, especially during difficult times. Remind yourself regularly of why you began your journey and what you hope to accomplish. This sense of purpose can fuel your resilience and keep you motivated.

4. **Embrace the Growth Mindset**: Cultivating a growth mindset, the belief that abilities and intelligence can improve with effort, strengthens perseverance. Viewing challenges as opportunities for growth reinforces resilience and maintains motivation to keep working toward long-term goals.

The journeys of notable individuals exemplify grit's power to transform lives and create lasting impact. J.K. Rowling faced numerous rejections from publishers before she finally succeeded in publishing *Harry Potter*, a series that would go on to shape a generation. Her resilience and unwavering passion for storytelling drove her through periods of doubt and financial difficulty.

Thomas Edison is another classic example of perseverance and grit. Known for inventing the light bulb, Edison reportedly failed thousands of times before succeeding. Instead of seeing these failures as setbacks, Edison viewed them as learning experiences, famously stating, "I have not failed. I've just found 10,000 ways that won't work." His unrelenting determination not only led to his success but has inspired countless others to adopt a similarly resilient mindset.

Through cultivating perseverance and grit, one can unlock their potential to achieve success beyond what they may have thought possible. These traits empower people to weather life's inevitable storms and emerge stronger, wiser, and more resilient.

Embracing Failure as a Learning Opportunity

Failure is often viewed as a sign of inadequacy or defeat, but with the right perspective, it can become a powerful stepping stone toward growth and success. Carol Dweck's work on the "growth mindset" highlights the importance of reframing failure as an opportunity for learning rather than as a setback. Dweck argues that people with a growth mindset—who believe that intelligence and abilities can be developed—are more likely to embrace challenges and learn from their mistakes. By seeing failure as feedback rather than a final verdict, individuals and leaders can harness it to fuel continuous improvement.

Redefining Failure

Failure, when redefined as feedback, allows us to understand what didn't work and why. This shift in perspective turns setbacks into invaluable learning experiences. Dweck's research shows that when we view challenges as growth opportunities, we become more resilient and willing to take calculated risks. For leaders, this mindset shift is crucial; it enables them to stay open to new possibilities, even after experiencing setbacks. The journey from failure to success often requires perseverance, adaptability, and a commitment to learning from each attempt.

Common Mistakes in Handling Failure

Despite the potential for growth, many leaders struggle to handle failure constructively. Some avoid taking accountability, shifting blame onto others, while others may refuse to reflect deeply on what went wrong. These reactions can hinder growth and prevent them from seeing the bigger picture. Honest self-reflection, however, is an invaluable tool for turning failure into progress. Leaders who admit their mistakes and assess them transparently not only build trust within their teams but also foster a culture of continuous learning. To create this environment, leaders must be willing to acknowledge their mistakes and focus on improvement rather than defensiveness.

Framework for Learning from Failure

A structured approach to learning from failure can help turn negative experiences into growth. One effective framework includes three steps: reflect, analyze, and adjust.

1. **Reflect**: Begin by acknowledging the failure without judgment. Reflect on the experience and identify the key moments and decisions that contributed to the outcome.

2. **Analyze**: Break down the elements of the failure to understand why it happened. Analyze patterns, assumptions, or choices that might have led to the mistake.

3. **Adjust**: Make a plan to apply the lessons learned. Adjust your approach, develop new strategies, or acquire additional skills if needed. This step ensures that each failure becomes a stepping stone toward improvement.

Techniques for Maintaining Mental Resilience

To maintain mental resilience, leaders can implement several techniques that support mental strength and clarity:

1. **Mindfulness and Meditation**: Mindfulness helps leaders stay calm and focused, even under stress. Simple meditation practices, such as deep breathing or focused attention on sensations, enable leaders to clear their minds and reduce stress. To start, set aside five minutes daily, sit comfortably, close your eyes, and focus on your breath. Benefits include reduced anxiety, increased focus, and improved emotional regulation.

2. **Physical Well-being**: Physical health is foundational to mental resilience. Regular exercise releases endorphins, which boost mood, while quality sleep restores cognitive function and supports stress management. A balanced diet provides necessary nutrients that improve mental clarity and energy. Aim for at least 30 minutes of exercise, seven to eight hours of sleep, and a nutritious diet to enhance resilience.

3. **Emotional Support Systems:** Building a support system of mentors, colleagues, or friends is crucial. These connections provide guidance, encouragement, and empathy. Sharing struggles fosters vulnerability and authentic connection, reinforcing resilience through shared experiences.

4. **Cognitive Strategies:** Techniques like cognitive reframing help shift perspectives to find positives in challenges. Visualization—mentally picturing successful outcomes—boosts confidence and motivation, empowering leaders to approach

challenges with a resilient mindset.

Leaders Who Thrived Despite Facing Adversity

1. Howard Schultz

Howard Schultz, former CEO of Starbucks, grew up in a struggling working-class family in Brooklyn, New York. Witnessing his father's hardships inspired him to create a company that prioritized employee well-being. Schultz envisioned Starbucks as a "third place" between work and home, providing a sense of community. However, he faced considerable challenges, including intense competition and economic downturns. Despite these obstacles, he led Starbucks through difficult times, including his return as CEO to revive the company during the 2008 financial crisis.

Lesson: Schultz's story teaches leaders the value of staying true to a mission, especially in the face of adversity, and the importance of empathy in leadership.

2. Oprah Winfrey

Oprah Winfrey's rise to success from a difficult childhood in poverty is a powerful example of resilience. Despite facing abuse and discrimination, she transformed her struggles into a deep empathy that became the foundation of her career. Building a media empire, she used her platform to connect with millions and advocate for self-improvement.

Her philosophy emphasizes finding purpose in pain and using challenges as motivation. **Lesson**: Oprah's journey highlights the importance of self-belief, vulnerability, and resilience, showing leaders that adversity can fuel a purpose-driven life.

3. Nelson Mandela

Nelson Mandela's life exemplifies resilience on a global scale. Imprisoned for 27 years due to his fight against apartheid, he maintained hope and mental strength, emerging not with bitterness but with a vision of reconciliation for South Africa. His endurance and commitment to justice made him a symbol of resilience, influencing change worldwide. **Lesson**: Mandela's legacy teaches that resilience is strengthened by a commitment to higher ideals, and that personal hardship can be transformed into powerful leadership.

4. Elon Musk

Elon Musk's ventures in SpaceX and Tesla were filled with failures and financial risks, nearly driving him to bankruptcy. His unyielding commitment to sustainable energy and space exploration kept him going even when others doubted him. Musk's persistence has revolutionized industries and inspired innovation. **Lesson**: Musk's journey underlines the need for leaders to maintain a clear vision, embrace failure, and persist despite setbacks, as resilience can pave the way to groundbreaking achievements.

Integrating Resilience into Leadership

In the journey toward effective leadership, resilience, grit, the ability to embrace failure, and mental toughness are indispensable. These traits not only strengthen personal resolve but also inspire teams to thrive amid challenges. Leaders must actively cultivate these qualities, seeing resilience as more than an individual asset but a shared team strength. Embracing resilience as a lifelong journey rather than a fixed trait challenges leaders to continuously adapt and grow. By committing to this path, they lay the foundation for resilient, empowered teams that are well-equipped to overcome obstacles and achieve lasting success.

Chapter 5

LEADING WITH INTEGRITY AND CHARACTER

In a 2019 global study by Edelman, 67% of employees stated that trust in leadership significantly influenced their job satisfaction and performance. Leadership integrity isn't just a lofty ideal; it's a fundamental pillar that determines the success and sustainability of any organization. Consider the story of Aaron Feuerstein, the former CEO of Malden Mills, who made headlines in 1995. After a devastating fire destroyed his textile factory, Feuerstein chose to continue paying his employees while rebuilding, despite financial strain. His actions were a testament to integrity and character, earning him admiration and loyalty from his team and the broader community.

Integrity in leadership refers to adhering to ethical principles and moral values, regardless of circumstances or external pressures. It is about doing the right thing, even when no one is watching. Character, on the other hand, encompasses the qualities that define a leader's moral and ethical compass, such as honesty, empathy, and accountability. Together, these traits create a foundation of trust, enabling leaders to inspire and guide their teams effectively.

Ethical leadership is not optional; it is essential. In today's complex world, where organizations face increasing scrutiny and employees demand transparency, leaders with strong moral grounding set the tone for a culture of trust, collaboration, and innovation. This chapter explores the principles of ethical leadership, the importance of honesty and transparency, and practical strategies for cultivating trust within teams. Through self-reflection and actionable exercises, readers will gain valuable insights to lead with integrity and character.

The Importance of Ethics and Strong Moral Grounding in Leadership

Ethics and moral grounding are essential pillars of effective leadership. Ethics can be defined as a set of principles that govern behavior, determining what is right and wrong. According to the *Oxford English Dictionary*, ethics involves "moral principles that govern a person's behavior or the conducting of an activity." Moral grounding refers to an individual's commitment to these principles, ensuring actions align with a strong sense of integrity and fairness. Together, they form the foundation for trust and credibility in leadership.

The Role of Ethics in Leadership

Ethical leadership is critical to fostering trust and a healthy organizational culture. Leaders who demonstrate integrity inspire confidence among team members, partners, and stakeholders. By setting clear examples of ethical behavior, these leaders encourage transparency, fairness, and accountability. For instance, ethical leaders prioritize open communication and empower their teams to voice concerns without fear of retaliation. This contributes to higher employee morale and fosters a sense of belonging within the organization.

Consequences of Unethical Leadership

Conversely, unethical leadership can have disastrous effects. Corporate scandals such as the collapse of Enron and the Volkswagen emissions scandal highlight the consequences of ethical lapses. Enron's executives engaged in fraudulent accounting practices, which led to the company's downfall in 2001 and the loss of thousands of jobs and pensions. Similarly, Volkswagen's manipulation of emissions tests in 2015 tarnished its reputation and resulted in billions of dollars in fines. These examples underscore how a lack of moral grounding erodes trust, damages brand equity, and causes long-term harm to employees and stakeholders.

Studies consistently demonstrate the positive impact of ethical leadership on organizational outcomes. Research published in the *Journal of Business Ethics* reveals that ethical leaders improve team performance, job satisfaction, and employee retention. For example, a 2022 study by Gallup found that employees are 30% less likely to leave organizations led by ethical leaders, and these organizations are 20% more profitable on average than their less ethical counterparts.

Principles of Ethical Leadership

Ethical leadership is essential for building trust, fostering collaboration, and creating a sustainable organizational culture. Leaders who adhere to ethical principles set a positive example and inspire their teams to do the same. Below are six key principles of ethical leadership, with examples and their real-life applications.

1.   Respect for Others

Respecting others means acknowledging their inherent worth, treating them with dignity, and considering their perspectives in decision-making. Ethical leaders value open communication, actively listen, and ensure that all team members feel heard.

Satya Nadella, CEO of Microsoft, emphasizes a "growth mindset" within his team, promoting respect and learning from one another. His leadership has fostered a collaborative and innovative culture at Microsoft. Treating people with respect encourages teamwork, minimizes conflicts, and boosts morale.

2.   Justice and Fairness

Justice and fairness require leaders to make decisions impartially and without favoritism. Ethical leaders ensure that policies are applied uniformly and equitably across all employees. Fair treatment builds trust, motivates employees, and creates an environment where everyone feels valued.

An example of fairness in leadership can be seen in Howard Schultz's tenure as CEO of Starbucks. Schultz implemented employee-friendly policies like comprehensive healthcare benefits for part-time workers, demonstrating fairness and care for employees at all levels. This equitable approach earned Starbucks a reputation as a great place to work and increased employee loyalty.

3.   Accountability

Accountability involves taking responsibility for one's actions, decisions, and outcomes, both positive and negative. Ethical leaders model accountability by admitting mistakes and working to rectify them rather than deflecting blame.

A notable example of accountability is when Johnson & Johnson acted decisively during the 1982 Tylenol tampering crisis. The company recalled millions of bottles of Tylenol, even at great financial cost, to ensure customer safety. This transparent and responsible response not only preserved public trust but also solidified the company's reputation for ethical behavior.

4.   Empathy and compassion

Empathy and compassion are essential for understanding and addressing the needs, concerns, and challenges of team members. By showing genuine care, leaders create a supportive environment that enhances employee well-being and productivity.

Arvind Krishna, CEO of IBM, demonstrated compassion during the COVID-19 pandemic by implementing flexible work policies and prioritizing employee health. By empathizing with the challenges faced by employees, IBM strengthened its relationship with its workforce, leading to higher engagement and satisfaction.

5.   Courage

Courageous leaders stand firm on ethical principles, even when faced with adversity or unpopularity. They make decisions based on what is right rather than what is easy or convenient.

For instance, Tim Cook, CEO of Apple, demonstrated courage when he publicly opposed government demands to unlock an iPhone in 2016, citing customer privacy concerns. Despite facing significant pressure, Cook upheld Apple's commitment to protecting user data. Such decisions highlight the importance of integrity and inspire trust in leadership.

6. Consistency

Consistency means that leaders align their actions with their words and ethical values. Leaders who consistently act with integrity build credibility and serve as role models for their teams.

An example of consistency is Patagonia founder Yvon Chouinard, who aligned the company's business practices with its environmental values. Patagonia consistently prioritizes sustainable practices, demonstrating its commitment to environmental stewardship. This consistency has earned the brand loyal customers and admiration worldwide.

Real-Life Application of Ethical Principles

Implementing these principles requires deliberate effort and self-awareness. Leaders should regularly assess their actions, seek feedback, and prioritize transparency. For example:

- Respect: Conduct regular team-building exercises to strengthen collaboration.

- Fairness: Establish clear guidelines to ensure impartiality in promotions and rewards.

- Accountability: Implement systems for tracking performance and learning from mistakes.

- Empathy: Schedule regular one-on-one meetings to understand team members' needs.

- Courage: Advocate for ethical policies, even in challenging circumstances.

- Consistency: Reinforce organizational values in daily decision-making.

The Role of Honesty and Transparency in Leadership

Honesty and transparency are essential qualities in leadership, forming the foundation for trust, effective communication, and organizational success. While closely related, these principles are distinct. Honesty involves truthfulness, integrity, and adherence to ethical principles in words and actions. Transparency, on the other hand, is the act of openly sharing information, intentions, and decisions with stakeholders. Together, they create an environment of openness and accountability, enabling leaders to foster trust and collaboration within their teams.

Benefits of Honesty and Transparency in Leadership

1. Enhanced Communication

Honest and transparent leaders promote clear and open dialogue, ensuring that employees feel informed and valued. This minimizes misunderstandings and promotes a culture of collaboration. Teams are more likely to align with organizational goals when leaders communicate openly and truthfully.

2. Increased Trust

Trust is a cornerstone of effective leadership. A 2020 study by *Harvard Business Review* found that employees are more likely to trust leaders who consistently demonstrate honesty and transparency. This trust translates into higher morale, loyalty, and productivity, as employees feel secure knowing their leaders operate with integrity.

3. Reduced Conflicts

Transparency reduces ambiguity, which is often a source of workplace conflict. By openly sharing decisions, policies, and rationales, leaders eliminate speculation and ensure that all stakeholders are on the same page.

4. **Better decision-making**

Transparent leaders engage employees in decision-making processes, encouraging diverse perspectives. This inclusion leads to more informed and balanced decisions that benefit the entire organization.

New Zealand's former Prime Minister Jacinda Ardern is an exemplary leader known for her honesty and transparency. During the COVID-19 pandemic, she provided clear and consistent updates, communicating complex decisions in an empathetic and straightforward manner. Her approach garnered widespread trust and global admiration for its effectiveness.

Challenges of Transparency and How to Overcome Them

1. Fear of vulnerability

Some leaders fear that transparency might expose weaknesses or invite criticism. Overcoming this challenge requires a shift in mindset—leaders must recognize that admitting challenges and seeking input is a sign of strength, not weakness.

2. Balancing confidentiality

While transparency is vital, certain information, such as sensitive financial data or personal employee details, must remain confidential. Leaders can address this by clearly defining what can and cannot be shared, ensuring openness without compromising privacy or security.

3. **Cultural Resistance**

In some organizational cultures, transparency may not be the norm, making it difficult for leaders to implement. Leaders can gradually introduce transparency by modeling the behavior, encouraging feedback, and demonstrating its benefits.

Below is a conceptual flowchart showing how honesty and transparency lead to trust and improved decision-making:

Honesty →Clear Communication → Trust

Transparency → Open Sharing of Information → Employee Involvement

Trust + Involvement → Stronger Team Cohesion + Better Decision-Making

Cultivating Trust Within Teams

Trust is the foundation of effective leadership and a critical driver of team cohesion, collaboration, and performance. When trust exists within a team, members feel secure, respected, and motivated to contribute their best efforts. Conversely, a lack of trust breeds uncertainty, miscommunication, and disengagement. Leaders play a pivotal role in cultivating and maintaining trust, which requires consistent effort, empathy, and accountability.

Why Trust is Critical

Trust is the glue that holds teams together. Research from the *Harvard Business Review* indicates that high-trust organizations experience 50% higher employee productivity, 74% lower stress levels, and 40% less burnout compared to low-trust organizations. Trust fosters psychological safety, enabling team members to share ideas, take risks, and innovate without fear of judgment or reprisal. A trusted leader creates an environment where individuals feel valued, leading to stronger relationships and better outcomes.

How to Build Trust

1. Delivering on Promises

Leaders must consistently follow through on commitments. Even small actions, such as meeting deadlines or addressing concerns promptly, demonstrate reliability. This builds confidence in a leader's integrity.

2. Actively listening to team members

Trust grows when leaders genuinely listen to their team. Active listening involves giving full attention, asking clarifying questions, and acknowledging team members' input. For example, leaders can hold regular check-ins to address concerns, show empathy, and validate employees' perspectives.

3. **Providing constructive feedback**

Feedback, when delivered constructively, reinforces trust. Leaders should focus on actionable suggestions while recognizing strengths. For instance, instead of merely criticizing missed deadlines, a leader might explore underlying issues and collaborate on solutions, fostering growth and trust.

4. **Encouraging Open Communication**

Creating an open environment where team members can voice their thoughts without fear of reprisal is essential. Transparent communication builds credibility and demonstrates that a leader values honesty. Leaders can promote openness by holding regular team meetings and encouraging anonymous feedback channels.

One compelling study by *PwC* found that 55% of employees believe trust in leadership is a top driver of workplace satisfaction. An example of trust-building leadership is Mary Barra, CEO of General Motors, who emphasized transparency and accountability when addressing GM's ignition switch crisis. By openly acknowledging mistakes and committing to resolving them, Barra rebuilt trust with employees, customers, and stakeholders.

Addressing Broken Trust

Despite one's best efforts, trust can occasionally be broken. To rebuild it, leaders should:

1. **Acknowledge the breach**: admit mistakes openly and take full responsibility without making excuses.

2. **Apologize Sincerely**: A heartfelt apology demonstrates humility and a commitment to making amends.

3. **Clarify Intentions**: Reassure team members by explaining the steps being taken to rectify the situation.

4. **Take Corrective Action**: Implement changes to prevent future lapses, such as revising policies or improving communication.

5. **Be Patient**: Rebuilding trust takes time, consistency, and effort to demonstrate renewed reliability.

Reflective Exercises on Personal Values and Ethics

Exploring personal values and ethics is essential for developing a strong foundation for leadership. Reflective exercises can help leaders identify their core beliefs, evaluate their alignment with their leadership style, and refine their decision-making approach. Below are three practical exercises designed to encourage self-awareness and growth.

1. Values Clarification Activity

Objective: Identify and prioritize core values that guide your leadership.

Instructions:

- Create a list of values such as honesty, accountability, empathy, fairness, and innovation.

- Select the top five values that resonate most with you.

- Reflect on how these values influence your leadership style. Example: If "empathy" is a core value, consider how you prioritize team well-being in decision-making.

Use a template (below) to record your reflections.

Template for Reflection:

Core Value	Why It's Important	How It Influences My Leadership
Example: Integrity	Ensures honesty in actions	Builds trust with my team
Add yours:		

2. Ethical dilemma scenarios

Objective: Practice ethical decision-making in challenging situations.

Scenario Example:

You discover that a high-performing employee has exaggerated their credentials on their resume. What would you do?

Option 1: Confront the employee privately to understand the situation.

Option 2: Inform HR immediately and follow company protocols.

Option 3: Overlook the issue to avoid disrupting team dynamics.

Reflection: Write down your choice and explain the reasoning behind it. Consider how your values influenced your decision.

3. Self-assessment questionnaire

Objective: Measure your ethical tendencies and identify areas for growth.

Instructions: Rate yourself on a scale of 1 (rarely) to 5 (always) for each statement below:

- I admit my mistakes and take responsibility for them.
- I make decisions based on fairness, not favoritism.

- I actively seek feedback from my team to improve.

- I prioritize honesty, even when it's difficult. I treat everyone with respect, regardless of their role.

Reflection: Total your score. Higher scores indicate strong ethical tendencies.

Identify one or two areas for improvement and set actionable goals.

Application in Leadership

Understanding your values and ethics directly impacts your leadership. When leaders align their actions with their core values, they build trust, credibility, and a consistent decision-making framework. For example, a leader who values accountability will readily admit mistakes, fostering a culture of transparency within their team.

In today's fast-paced and interconnected world, ethical leadership is not a luxury but a necessity. Throughout this discussion, we have explored the fundamental principles that define ethical leadership, including respect, fairness, accountability, empathy, and consistency. We've highlighted how honesty and transparency build trust, foster better communication, and enhance decision-making. Practical strategies and exercises were also presented to help leaders align their actions with their values and refine their ethical decision-making.

At the heart of ethical leadership lies integrity and character. Leading with these qualities creates a positive ripple effect, inspiring teams, building trust, and driving sustainable success. Leaders who prioritize ethics not only enhance organizational performance but also leave a lasting legacy of credibility and respect.

Now is the time to reflect on your leadership journey. Ask yourself: Are my actions aligned with my values? Do I inspire trust and transparency within my team? Ethical leadership begins with self-awareness and a commitment to growth.

Take a moment to review your core values, confront ethical dilemmas with courage, and strive for consistency in your decisions. By leading with integrity, you have the power to transform not only your organization but also the lives of those you serve. Start today—lead with purpose and inspire the change you wish to see.

Chapter 6

FOSTERING INNOVATION AND CREATIVITY

Innovation and creativity are the lifeblood of progress in any organization. They drive breakthroughs, solve complex problems, and keep businesses competitive in an ever-evolving world. Creativity is the ability to generate new and original ideas, while innovation is the process of turning those ideas into tangible solutions or advancements. In the words of Steve Jobs, the legendary co-founder of Apple, *"Innovation distinguishes between a leader and a follower."* This statement underscores the critical role leaders play in fostering environments where creativity and innovation thrive.

Great leaders are the architects of innovative cultures. They not only inspire individuals to think outside the box but also provide the tools, support, and freedom necessary to experiment and take calculated risks. Consider Satya Nadella, who transformed Microsoft by fostering a "growth mindset" culture. Under his leadership, Microsoft shifted from a competitive, siloed environment to one that values collaboration, curiosity, and experimentation. This cultural shift fueled groundbreaking innovations such as the rapid expansion of Microsoft Azure and the development of AI-powered tools.

The purpose of this chapter is to explore how exceptional leaders nurture creativity and innovation within their teams and organizations. It delves into three critical strategies: creating a culture that values creative thinking, supporting calculated risk-taking, and leveraging diversity to inspire fresh ideas. For example, Jeff Bezos, the founder of Amazon, has famously championed a culture of "customer obsession" and "willingness to fail." These principles have enabled Amazon to launch revolutionary products like the Kindle and Alexa, even in the face of uncertainty.

By examining how these leaders build environments that empower teams to think creatively and take bold steps, this chapter offers practical insights for aspiring leaders to implement in their own organizations. Whether you are leading a small team or a multinational corporation, fostering innovation and creativity is not merely an option—it is an imperative for sustained success in today's dynamic world.

How Great Leaders Encourage and Nurture Innovation

Innovation doesn't happen by accident—it requires intentional effort and the right leadership to flourish. Great leaders understand that their role is to inspire, support, and guide their teams in exploring uncharted territory. They create environments where creativity can thrive by fostering open communication, empowering teams, and emphasizing continuous learning. Through these strategies, leaders lay the foundation for groundbreaking ideas and solutions that propel organizations forward.

Encouragement of Open Communication

Innovation starts with the free flow of ideas. Great leaders recognize that creativity often emerges from collaboration and open dialogue. They cultivate environments where employees feel safe sharing their thoughts, even when those ideas challenge the status quo. This psychological safety, as highlighted by leadership expert Amy Edmondson, ensures that team members contribute without fear of criticism or judgment.

Google's "20% Time" policy is a prime example of this principle in action. Introduced by co-founders Larry Page and Sergey Brin, this policy allows employees to dedicate

20% of their time to passion projects that may not align with their primary job responsibilities. The result? Game-changing innovations such as Gmail, Google Maps, and Google News. By giving employees, the freedom to explore their ideas and creating a space where those ideas are valued, Google has consistently remained at the forefront of technological innovation.

To encourage open communication, leaders must also model the behavior they wish to see. Elon Musk, the CEO of Tesla and SpaceX, is known for his "open-door policy." He encourages employees at all levels to share ideas directly with him, bypassing hierarchical barriers. Musk once stated, *"I do think there's a good framework for thinking. It's physics. You reason from first principles rather than by analogy."* His focus on foundational thinking inspires employees to voice original ideas and approach problems creatively.

Empowering Teams

Empowering teams means giving them the autonomy, trust, and resources needed to innovate. Great leaders understand that micromanagement stifles creativity, while trust enables teams to take ownership of their work and experiment with new approaches. When employees feel empowered, they are more likely to push boundaries and develop novel solutions.

Satya Nadella's transformation of Microsoft illustrates the power of empowerment. When Nadella became CEO in 2014, he inherited a company that was losing relevance in the tech industry. He quickly shifted Microsoft's culture to embrace a "growth mindset," a concept popularized by psychologist Carol Dweck. Nadella encouraged employees to focus on learning, collaboration, and experimentation rather than fear of failure. Under his leadership, Microsoft moved away from rigid hierarchies and embraced a culture where teams were empowered to take risks and experiment. This approach led to innovations such as the growth of Microsoft Azure, the company's cloud computing platform, and the integration of AI across its products.

Empowerment also involves providing teams with the tools and resources they need to succeed. Howard Schultz, the former CEO of Starbucks, famously empowered his teams by prioritizing employee well-being. He introduced comprehensive healthcare benefits and tuition reimbursement programs, ensuring that employees felt supported both personally and professionally. This investment in employees fostered a sense of loyalty and creativity, enabling Starbucks to continually innovate its customer experience.

Emphasizing Continuous Learning

The most innovative leaders understand that learning is a lifelong process. They encourage their teams to stay curious, explore new trends, and continuously develop their skills. By fostering a culture of learning, leaders ensure their organizations remain adaptable and forward-thinking in the face of change.

Elon Musk exemplifies this principle with his relentless pursuit of knowledge. Known for teaching himself rocket science to found SpaceX, Musk frequently emphasizes the importance of interdisciplinary learning. He encourages his teams to draw inspiration from fields outside their expertise. For instance, Tesla's engineers have applied principles from material science, artificial intelligence, and even neuroscience to develop cutting-edge technologies like self-driving cars and battery innovations. Musk's passion for learning and innovation is infectious, motivating his teams to think beyond conventional limits.

Another example is Amazon's "Leadership Principles," which include "Learn and Be Curious." This principle encourages employees to seek out new ideas and expand their knowledge. Jeff Bezos, the company's founder, has said, *"If you double the number of experiments you do per year, you're going to double your inventiveness."* This focus on learning has led Amazon to continuously disrupt industries, from e-commerce to cloud computing.

Creating a Culture That Values Creative Thinking

An organization's success in fostering innovation depends on its culture—a collective set of values, behaviors, and attitudes that shape how employees think and act. Leaders play a pivotal role in building a culture where creativity is not just encouraged but celebrated. By establishing a vision for creativity, encouraging experimentation, providing the right tools, and recognizing and rewarding innovation, leaders can ensure their organizations remain dynamic and forward-thinking.

Establishing a Vision for Creativity

The foundation of a creative culture begins with a clear and compelling vision from leadership. Great leaders articulate how creativity aligns with the organization's mission and goals, embedding it into the company's DNA. This vision serves as a guiding principle, inspiring employees to think beyond the ordinary and explore innovative solutions.

For example, Walt Disney's vision for his company was simple yet profound: to create a place where imagination could come to life. By prioritizing storytelling and creativity, Disney established a culture that encouraged employees to push boundaries in animation, theme park design, and entertainment. This vision continues to inspire employees at Disney today, fostering groundbreaking projects like Pixar's cutting-edge animations and Disney+.

A vision for creativity must also address challenges and opportunities unique to the organization. Leaders like Indra Nooyi, the former CEO of PepsiCo, integrated creativity into the company's strategy by emphasizing "performance with purpose." Under her leadership, PepsiCo developed healthier, innovative products in response to changing consumer demands, demonstrating how a visionary approach can inspire transformative solutions.

Encouraging Experimentation

Experimentation is the lifeblood of creativity. Leaders who encourage their teams to test new ideas and accept failure as part of the process cultivate a culture where innovation thrives. The most creative companies understand that success often arises from multiple failures and view setbacks as valuable learning opportunities rather than deterrents.

Amazon is a prime example of an organization that embraces experimentation. Jeff Bezos, Amazon's founder, famously stated, **"Failure and invention are inseparable twins."** This philosophy was evident in the development of the Fire Phone, a smartphone launched by Amazon in 2014. Despite its commercial failure, the lessons learned from the Fire Phone's development directly contributed to the creation of Amazon Echo and Alexa, products that revolutionized voice-assisted technology. By encouraging experimentation and accepting the potential for failure, Amazon continually pushes the boundaries of innovation.

Leaders can foster a culture of experimentation by creating a "safe-to-fail" environment where employees are encouraged to propose bold ideas without fear of retribution. When employees know their efforts will be valued, even if unsuccessful, they are more likely to take risks and explore uncharted territory.

Providing Tools and Resources

A culture of creativity flourishes when employees have access to the tools, resources, and methodologies they need to innovate. Leaders must invest in both tangible and intangible resources to enable teams to think and act creatively.

Cutting-edge tools, such as collaboration software, can streamline the process of brainstorming and innovation.

Companies like Slack, Zoom, and Miro provide platforms for teams to share ideas in real time, regardless of geographic location. Additionally, methodologies like Design Thinking have proven to be powerful frameworks for fostering creativity. Design Thinking workshops, often used by companies such as IDEO, help teams approach problems from a human-centered perspective. By focusing on empathy, ideation, and rapid prototyping, these workshops generate innovative solutions that address real-world challenges.

IDEO, a global design and consulting firm, has built its entire culture around tools and techniques that spark creativity. For example, during the redesign of a hospital emergency room, IDEO employed Design Thinking to understand the needs of patients, doctors, and nurses. By providing their team with the structure and tools to explore the problem, they delivered a groundbreaking solution that improved patient experience and workflow efficiency.

Beyond tools, leaders can support creativity by fostering an environment conducive to deep work and collaboration. For example, companies like Google provide flexible workspaces, including "quiet zones" for focus and open areas for brainstorming. These physical and digital resources empower employees to think creatively and execute their ideas effectively.

Recognizing and Rewarding Innovation

Acknowledgment and rewards are powerful motivators in a culture of creativity. When employees see their innovative efforts recognized, they feel valued and inspired to continue contributing to the organization's success.

Leaders who prioritize recognition ensure that achievements, both big and small, are celebrated. For instance, at 3M, a company renowned for its culture of innovation, employees are recognized and rewarded for developing successful products. One of 3M's most famous innovations, the Post-it Note, emerged from an employee's accidental discovery of a low-tack adhesive. Instead of dismissing the idea, the company recognized its potential and celebrated its creator, fostering an environment where such "happy accidents" are encouraged.

Recognition doesn't always have to be monetary. Public acknowledgment, promotions, and opportunities for growth can also serve as effective rewards. Leaders like Satya Nadella have emphasized the importance of creating opportunities for employees who demonstrate creative thinking. At Microsoft, Nadella has introduced programs that showcase employees' innovative projects to the entire company, creating a ripple effect of inspiration.

Additionally, organizations can formalize rewards for creativity through initiatives like innovation awards or dedicated innovation programs. For example, Adobe's "Kickbox" program provides employees with a toolkit and funding to experiment with new ideas. By supporting employees in this way, Adobe encourages a mindset of ownership and exploration, reinforcing the value of creativity.

Supporting Calculated Risk-Taking

In the pursuit of creativity and innovation, risk-taking is unavoidable. However, not all risks lead to success, and the difference lies in how those risks are approached. Great leaders understand that fostering creativity requires embracing calculated risks—decisions that are informed, analyzed, and balanced with potential outcomes. By encouraging thoughtful risk-taking, leaders create an environment where their teams feel empowered to innovate without fear of failure. This section explores the nuances of calculated risks and the leadership strategies that support them.

Defining Calculated Risks

Calculated risks differ fundamentally from reckless decisions. While reckless risks are impulsive and lack proper evaluation, calculated risks involve thorough analysis, weighing potential outcomes, and making informed choices. Leaders who support calculated risks encourage their teams to evaluate scenarios, consider alternatives, and plan for contingencies before acting.

One clear example of calculated risk-taking is SpaceX's decision to launch reusable rockets, an idea that was initially met with skepticism. Elon Musk and his team meticulously analyzed the potential benefits and challenges of reusability, conducting extensive simulations and iterative testing. While the process involved high stakes and significant failures along the way, their calculated approach ultimately led to groundbreaking advancements in space travel. This demonstrates how taking risks—when backed by data and planning—can yield transformative results.

Creating a Safe-to-Fail Environment

Innovation flourishes in environments where failure is not stigmatized but embraced as part of the creative process. Leaders who create a "safe-to-fail" culture empower their teams to experiment with new ideas without fear of harsh consequences. They frame failure as a stepping stone to success, helping employees view setbacks as valuable learning opportunities.

In practice, creating a safe-to-fail environment requires consistent messaging and supportive actions. For instance, Google encourages teams to celebrate their "moonshots," even when those ambitious projects don't succeed. This culture has led to extraordinary achievements, such as Google Maps and self-driving cars, while minimizing the fear of failure that can stifle innovation.

Teaching Risk Assessment

One of the most effective ways leaders can support calculated risk-taking is by teaching their teams how to assess and manage risks. By equipping employees with tools to evaluate potential outcomes, leaders help them make informed decisions while still encouraging bold ideas.

Jeff Bezos, uses the "Regret Minimization Framework" as a decision-making tool. Bezos explained that when faced with a risky decision, he asks himself, *"Will I regret not doing this when I'm 80?"* This framework encourages long-term thinking, focusing on opportunities rather than short-term fears. This philosophy led to Amazon's entry into the e-commerce market, its creation of AWS (Amazon Web Services), and the launch of Kindle—all of which were calculated risks that paid off immensely.

Leaders can implement structured risk assessment practices, such as SWOT analysis (Strengths, Weaknesses, Opportunities, Threats), to help teams evaluate projects. By fostering a mindset of preparation and strategic thinking, leaders ensure that risks are taken with clarity and confidence.

Balancing Risk with Accountability

While encouraging calculated risks, leaders must also maintain a balance by establishing clear accountability. Creative freedom without accountability can lead to chaos, while excessive control can stifle innovation. Striking the right balance ensures that risks are taken responsibly and that teams learn from both successes and failures.

Accountability can be established through clear goal-setting and feedback mechanisms. For example, leaders might set specific objectives for innovative projects, track progress through measurable metrics, and regularly review outcomes. Pixar Animation Studios exemplifies this approach by conducting "post-mortems" after every film project. These sessions analyze what worked, what didn't, and how future projects can improve. By holding teams accountable in a constructive way, Pixar fosters continuous learning while maintaining high standards.

Leaders must also communicate expectations about risk-taking. A leader might say, *"I expect you to take risks, but I also expect you to show me how you've thought it through."* This approach combines encouragement with accountability, ensuring that risks are pursued responsibly.

Leveraging Diversity to Inspire New Ideas

Diversity is a catalyst for creativity. By bringing together individuals with different backgrounds, experiences, and perspectives, leaders can create a dynamic environment where new ideas flourish. Diversity enriches problem-solving, fosters innovation, and helps organizations stay competitive in a rapidly evolving world. Great leaders recognize this potential and intentionally build inclusive, diverse teams to drive creativity and generate breakthrough solutions.

Diversity in Teams

Innovation thrives when teams combine varied skills, perspectives, and expertise. Diverse teams are better equipped to tackle complex challenges, as each member brings a unique approach to solving problems. Research from McKinsey has shown that companies with more diverse teams are significantly more likely to outperform their peers in innovation and financial performance.

A notable example of leveraging diversity for innovation is Apple's development of the original iPhone. Steve Jobs intentionally brought together a cross-functional team of hardware engineers, software developers, and industrial designers with varied expertise to create a revolutionary product. This collaboration produced a device that seamlessly integrated hardware and software, combining innovation from multiple disciplines into a single, user-friendly design. By fostering diversity within its development teams, Apple disrupted the mobile phone market and set a new standard for technology.

Leaders can emulate this approach by assembling teams with complementary skills and encouraging open collaboration across departments. When diverse perspectives are embraced, the result is often more innovative solutions and transformative ideas.

Leadership Practices

While diversity is essential, it must be accompanied by inclusive leadership practices that ensure every voice is heard. Inclusive leaders actively create spaces where underrepresented groups feel valued, empowered, and encouraged to contribute their ideas. This not only amplifies the potential for innovation but also ensures equity within the decision-making process.

Indra Nooyi, the former CEO of PepsiCo, demonstrated the power of inclusivity in driving creativity. Under her leadership, PepsiCo emphasized the value of diverse talent by creating products that catered to various cultural and demographic preferences. For example, Nooyi introduced healthier snack options tailored to global markets, leveraging insights from employees with diverse cultural backgrounds. Her inclusive leadership style encouraged employees to share their unique perspectives, resulting in innovative products that resonated with a broader customer base.

To replicate this, leaders must actively seek out contributions from diverse team members and address barriers that may prevent participation. Strategies such as mentorship programs for underrepresented groups and inclusive brainstorming sessions can amplify these voices and unlock untapped potential.

Cross-Cultural Inspiration

In a globalized world, exposure to diverse cultures and markets fuels creativity by challenging assumptions and broadening perspectives. Companies that embrace cross-cultural inspiration are better positioned to innovate in ways that resonate with a wide audience.

Airbnb offers an excellent example of cross-cultural creativity. Recognizing that hospitality preferences vary widely across countries, Airbnb leveraged insights from its global user base to design personalized experiences. By studying how different cultures approach hospitality—whether it's Japanese minimalism or the warmth of Brazilian host traditions—Airbnb refined its platform to cater to diverse travelers' needs. This cultural awareness not only strengthened its brand but also revolutionized how people experience travel.

Leaders can encourage cross-cultural inspiration by exposing teams to international markets, fostering collaborations across global offices, or even incorporating cultural immersion programs. These experiences challenge teams to think beyond their usual frame of reference, sparking innovative ideas influenced by diverse traditions and practices.

Avoiding Groupthink

Diversity also helps organizations avoid the pitfalls of groupthink, a phenomenon where homogeneity of thought stifles creativity. When team members share similar backgrounds or perspectives, they are more likely to conform to dominant ideas, limiting the scope of innovation. To counteract this, leaders must intentionally create an environment where differing opinions are not only welcomed but actively sought.

One effective strategy is to assign roles like "devil's advocate" during brainstorming sessions to ensure ideas are critically evaluated from multiple angles. Encouraging debate and alternative viewpoints fosters a culture of constructive disagreement, which leads to better decision-making and more creative solutions. For example, Amazon's leadership encourages teams to "disagree and commit," a practice that promotes rigorous discussion while maintaining unity in execution.

Leaders can also introduce diverse perspectives by inviting external advisors or consultants to challenge assumptions and provide fresh viewpoints. This strategy not only prevents groupthink but also broadens the team's understanding of potential solutions.

Examples of Innovative Leaders and Their Approaches

Innovation thrives under visionary leadership. Steve Jobs (Apple) prioritized simplicity and user-centric design, blending technology with the humanities to create groundbreaking products like the iPhone. His relentless pursuit of elegance and functionality revolutionized industries and demonstrated that understanding human needs drives innovation.

Elon Musk (Tesla, SpaceX) exemplifies bold, risk-taking leadership. His boundary-pushing vision for sustainable energy and space exploration has redefined industries. Musk's "first principles" approach—breaking problems into their most basic truths—enabled innovations like reusable rockets and electric vehicles, proving that calculated risks can lead to extraordinary results.

Sheryl Sandberg (Meta) fosters creativity through psychological safety, open communication, and inclusivity. Her leadership ensures diverse voices are heard, empowering teams to innovate collaboratively. Sandberg's emphasis on mentorship and transparency has been crucial in Meta's success.

Howard Schultz (Starbucks) transformed the coffee industry by focusing on the customer experience and employee well-being. His "third place" concept and innovative benefits for employees fostered loyalty, creating a thriving business model.

Arianna Huffington (Thrive Global) redefined workplace innovation by prioritizing well-being. Her initiatives combat stress and burnout, proving creativity flourishes in healthy environments.

These leaders highlight that fostering innovation requires bold ideas, inclusivity, and a commitment to human-centric approaches.

In conclusion, fostering innovation and creativity within leadership is not just a strategy—it is a necessity in today's fast-paced and ever-changing world. Leaders who prioritize these qualities inspire their teams to think outside the box, challenge the status quo, and envision solutions beyond conventional limits. By creating an environment that encourages creative thinking, leaders lay the groundwork for groundbreaking ideas and continuous improvement. Moreover, when leaders embrace calculated risks, they demonstrate the importance of stepping out of comfort zones, which can lead to extraordinary breakthroughs and growth.

A critical aspect of innovative leadership is embracing diversity in all its forms—thought, experience, and background. Leaders who cultivate diverse teams benefit from a broader range of perspectives, which enhances problem-solving and leads to more well-rounded decision-making. By empowering individuals from different walks of life, leaders tap into untapped potential and foster an atmosphere where unique ideas can flourish.

Ultimately, the role of a leader is to create a culture where creativity is not only valued but expected. As a leader, you have the opportunity to shape the mindset and direction of your team. Your leadership style can either stifle or spark innovation—it's up to you to set the tone. By embracing creativity, taking calculated risks, and fostering an inclusive environment, you can transform challenges into opportunities and inspire your team to reach new heights.

As you continue your leadership journey, remember that the most impactful leaders are those who challenge their teams to think creatively and act boldly. By adopting these practices, you will not only elevate your leadership skills but also create a legacy of innovation that will resonate for years to come.

Chapter 7

DEVELOPING AND EMPOWERING OTHERS

Leadership is the ability to influence, guide, and inspire others toward achieving a shared vision. At its core, leadership transcends authority—it thrives on fostering team growth and empowerment. Empowerment involves enabling individuals to realize their potential, take ownership of their roles, and contribute meaningfully to organizational goals. These qualities are pivotal for leaders aiming to cultivate innovative, resilient teams that thrive in dynamic environments.

Notable leaders throughout history have emphasized the importance of empowering others. For instance, Mahatma Gandhi once said, *"The best way to find yourself is to lose yourself in the service of others,"* underscoring the value of leading by example and inspiring collective growth. Similarly, business magnate Richard Branson advocates for delegation and trust, stating, *"If you take care of your employees, they will take care of your business."*

This chapter explores how leaders with a growth-oriented mindset recognize and cultivate individual strengths, delegate effectively, and use coaching techniques to empower their teams and amplify their leadership impact. By delving into these principles, it demonstrates how true leadership lies in enabling others to shine and achieve their best.

The Mindset of a Leader Who Prioritizes Team Growth

A growth-oriented mindset is a hallmark of effective leadership, characterized by a commitment to nurturing the potential of team members while striving for long-term success rather than immediate, short-term results. Leaders who prioritize team growth recognize that their success is inherently tied to the development of those they lead. By fostering an environment that encourages learning, innovation, and collaboration, such leaders ensure sustainable organizational growth and a more engaged workforce.

Empathy and vision are central to this mindset. Empathy allows leaders to understand and address the unique needs, aspirations, and challenges of their team members. Vision enables them to align individual goals with organizational objectives. As Nelson Mandela once said, *"It is better to lead from behind and to put others in front... when you celebrate victory, it will be because of them."* His words emphasize the importance of putting people first and empowering them to contribute meaningfully.

Leaders who prioritize growth also commit to their own continuous learning. By embracing new ideas and improving their skills, they set an example for their teams to follow. Satya Nadella, exemplifies this approach, stating, *"Don't be a know-it-all; be a learn-it-all."* His leadership transformed Microsoft's culture into one centered on curiosity, resilience, and adaptability.

Key traits such as humility, emotional intelligence, and collaboration underpin a growth-oriented mindset. Humility ensures that leaders value the contributions of others and acknowledge their own limitations. Emotional intelligence fosters trust and strengthens interpersonal relationships, while collaboration encourages collective success over individual accolades. As renowned coach John Wooden said, *"It is amazing how much can be accomplished if no one cares who gets the credit."*

Recognizing And Cultivating Individual Strengths

Effective leadership hinges on a leader's ability to recognize and nurture the unique strengths of their team members. By understanding individual talents and aligning them with organizational goals, leaders create an environment where both the team and the organization thrive. This requires active listening, observation, and continuous feedback to uncover what motivates individuals and where their abilities truly shine.

Understanding Team Members

Identifying individual strengths begins with building relationships founded on trust and open communication. Leaders who engage in active listening can uncover insights about their team members' preferences, aspirations, and areas of expertise. For example, Indra Nooyi, the former CEO of PepsiCo, often credited her leadership success to her ability to genuinely listen and understand her team. She believed that personalized attention not only revealed unique strengths but also inspired loyalty and confidence.

Observation is equally critical. By watching how team members approach their tasks and interact with others, leaders can identify natural talents, problem-solving abilities, and leadership potential. Complementing this with constructive feedback fosters a growth mindset, allowing team members to build on their strengths.

Strength-Based Assignments

Assigning roles and responsibilities that align with individual strengths is a powerful way to boost productivity, engagement, and job satisfaction. A team member with strong analytical skills, for example, may excel in data-driven decision-making roles, while a creative thinker might thrive in brainstorming and designing tasks. As Marcus Buckingham and Donald Clifton argue in *Now, Discover Your Strengths*, focusing on what people do best and encouraging them to cultivate those strengths leads to higher performance and fulfillment.

When leaders embrace this approach, they can also mitigate burnout by ensuring individuals are working in areas where they naturally excel. As Richard Branson said, *"Train people well enough so they can leave; treat them well enough so they don't want to."* Matching talent with opportunity ensures team members remain motivated and invested in their roles.

Encouraging Professional Development

Empowering team members involves providing opportunities for continuous learning. Training sessions, workshops, mentorship programs, and stretch assignments allow individuals to refine existing skills and acquire new ones. Stretch assignments, in particular, challenge team members to step outside their comfort zones, fostering growth and resilience. Leaders like Sheryl Sandberg, former COO of Meta, advocate for mentorship and learning opportunities, noting that *"leadership is not about titles, positions, or flowcharts. It is about one life influencing another."*

Celebrating Diversity

A diverse set of strengths brings innovation and adaptability to teams. By valuing and leveraging these differences, leaders can foster creative problem-solving and inclusivity. For example, Satya Nadella revitalized Microsoft by cultivating a culture that celebrated varied perspectives and empowered teams to think differently. Leaders who embrace diversity not only unlock their team's full potential but also build a more dynamic and robust organization. By recognizing and cultivating individual strengths, leaders inspire their teams to achieve excellence while creating an environment of trust, growth, and empowerment.

Delegating Effectively to Build Trust and Autonomy

Delegation is a cornerstone of effective leadership, enabling leaders to empower their teams while focusing on strategic priorities. By entrusting team members with meaningful responsibilities, leaders demonstrate confidence in their abilities and foster a sense of autonomy. Delegation not only enhances team productivity but also cultivates an environment of trust and growth, allowing individuals to develop their skills and take ownership of their work.

Why delegation matters

Empowering team members through delegation is a powerful way to enhance their confidence and capability. When leaders assign significant tasks, it shows that they trust their team to deliver. As former President Theodore Roosevelt once said, *"The best executive is the one who has sense enough to pick good men to do what he wants done and self-restraint enough to keep from meddling while they do it."* Effective delegation is about empowering others, not micromanaging them.

Delegation also benefits the leader, freeing them to focus on higher-level responsibilities while leveraging the diverse strengths within their team. Richard Branson, founder of the Virgin Group, famously credited delegation as a critical factor in his success, saying, *"If somebody can do something better than me, I get them to do it."*

Effective Delegation Strategies

For delegation to be successful, leaders must adopt practical and thoughtful strategies:

1. **Clearly define roles and expectations**: Team members perform best when they have a clear understanding of their responsibilities, goals, and deadlines. Providing

specific instructions ensures alignment and minimizes confusion.

2. **Match tasks to strengths**: Assigning tasks that align with individual skills ensures greater productivity and engagement. This strategy builds on the principles of strength-based leadership, where employees excel when they work in areas where they are most capable.

3. **Provide Resources and Support**: Empowerment doesn't mean abandonment. Effective leaders equip their teams with the tools, guidance, and feedback necessary to succeed. Regular check-ins can help address challenges without undermining autonomy.

Trust and Accountability

Delegation fosters trust when leaders allow team members to take full ownership of their assignments. By giving them the freedom to execute tasks their way, leaders show confidence in their judgment. This sense of trust, in turn, motivates employees to deliver high-quality work and strengthens their commitment to the team's success.

Simultaneously, accountability is essential for building a culture of responsibility. Leaders can reinforce accountability by setting clear expectations, celebrating successes, and constructively addressing setbacks. As Stephen R. Covey observed in *The 7 Habits of Highly*

Effective People, "Trust is the glue of life. It's the most essential ingredient in effective communication. It's the foundational principle that holds all relationships."

Through effective delegation, leaders empower their teams to grow, innovate, and contribute to organizational success while building strong bonds of trust and mutual respect.

Coaching and Mentorship Techniques

Leadership that prioritizes team empowerment often involves a combination of coaching and mentorship. While these approaches share the goal of fostering individual and team growth, they differ in focus and application. Coaching emphasizes performance improvement through skill-building and problem-solving, while mentorship provides long-term guidance by sharing wisdom, experience, and career advice. Together, coaching and mentorship equip team members with the tools and mindset to excel professionally and personally.

Coaching vs. Mentorship

Coaching is a structured process aimed at addressing specific goals or challenges. It focuses on enhancing performance and unlocking potential through tailored strategies. Mentorship, on the other hand, is relational and developmental, offering holistic guidance that spans career trajectory, personal growth, and broader life lessons. As

Eric Parsloe, a prominent coach and author, noted, *"Coaching is unlocking a person's potential to maximize their own performance. It is helping them to learn rather than teaching them.*

Mentorship, by contrast, often involves sharing personal experiences and offering advice to help mentees navigate their journeys. Leaders who embrace both methods can address immediate needs through coaching while nurturing long-term development through mentorship.

Key Coaching Techniques

1. **Active listening and open-ended questioning**: Active listening ensures that the coachee feels heard and understood, which builds trust and encourages open dialogue. Asking open-ended questions such as "What do you think is the best way to approach this?" promotes critical thinking and self-reflection. This approach shifts the focus to empowering individuals to find solutions.

2. **Setting SMART Goals**: A practical coaching framework involves setting SMART goals—Specific, Measurable, Achievable, Relevant, and Time-bound. This ensures that objectives are clearly defined, attainable, and aligned with both individual and organizational priorities.

3. **Providing constructive feedback:** Feedback is essential for improvement. Constructive feedback highlights

strengths while identifying areas for growth in a way that motivates rather than discourages. Leaders like Bill Gates have emphasized the value of feedback, famously saying, *"We all need people who will give us feedback. That's how we improve."*

Mentorship Approaches

Mentorship involves guiding individuals by sharing personal experiences and insights, helping them envision and pursue their long-term aspirations. Mentors play a critical role in broadening perspectives, offering advice, and fostering a sense of purpose. For example, Oprah Winfrey often credits her mentor, Maya Angelou, for shaping her outlook on leadership and life. Angelou's advice, *"When you learn, teach. When you get, give"* encapsulates the spirit of mentorship as an investment in others.

Effective mentors also focus on fostering independence and encouraging mentees to take initiative and explore their potential. By celebrating successes and navigating challenges together, mentors cultivate resilience and confidence in their mentees.

Incorporating coaching and mentorship into leadership practices empowers people to achieve their best, driving personal and organizational success.

How Empowering Others Strengthens Leadership Impact

Empowering others is a transformative leadership approach that amplifies a leader's impact while driving individual, team, and organizational success. By fostering trust, ownership, and innovation, leaders who empower their teams create a ripple effect of positivity and productivity that benefits everyone involved.

Ripple Effect of Empowerment

When leaders empower their teams, they unlock potential and inspire greater engagement, motivation, and innovation. Empowered team members feel valued and are more likely to take initiative and contribute meaningfully. This dynamic cultivates a sense of purpose and encourages employees to think creatively and solve problems independently. As Simon Sinek said, "Leadership is not about being in charge. It is about taking care of those in your charge." By prioritizing empowerment, leaders foster a culture of mutual respect and high morale, leading to better outcomes for the entire team.

Building future leaders

Empowerment plays a crucial role in developing future leaders. When leaders invest in their team's growth and provide opportunities to take on responsibilities, they cultivate leadership qualities like accountability, decision-making, and resilience. This approach builds a culture where leadership is shared, ensuring continuity and long-term success for the organization. Indra Nooyi emphasized this by stating, "Leadership is hard to define, and good leadership even harder. But if you can get people to follow you to the ends of the earth, you are a great leader." Empowering others ensures a pipeline of skilled, motivated individuals ready to step into leadership roles.

Enhanced leadership credibility

Empowering others strengthens a leader's credibility by demonstrating trust, humility, and confidence. Leaders who focus on enabling their teams to succeed are perceived as trustworthy, approachable, and capable. This fosters loyalty and respect, which in turn enhances the leader's ability to influence and inspire.

Organizational Benefits

The impact of empowerment extends beyond individual and team levels to benefit the organization as a whole. Empowered employees are more likely to stay engaged, leading to higher retention rates and lower turnover. Additionally, organizations with empowered teams see improved performance as motivated individuals collaborate more effectively and innovate more freely. Research consistently shows that organizations fostering empowerment experience stronger financial performance and higher employee satisfaction.

In essence, empowering others magnifies a leader's impact by cultivating engaged teams, developing future leaders, and driving organizational excellence.

As we have seen, empowering leadership is a dynamic and transformative approach that creates a ripple effect of growth and success. Leaders who prioritize a growth-oriented mindset, recognize and cultivate individual strengths, delegate effectively, and employ coaching and mentoring techniques foster an environment where teams thrive and innovation flourish. By focusing on empowerment, leaders enable their team members to take ownership, build confidence, and develop leadership qualities, ensuring long-term personal and organizational success.

Aspiring leaders are encouraged to embrace these practices, not only to achieve better results but also to inspire others to realize their potential. Empowerment is not about relinquishing control but about creating opportunities for shared growth and collective excellence. Leaders who champion these values will find their impact amplified, their teams more resilient, and their organizations positioned for sustained success.

As John Quincy Adams aptly stated, "If your actions inspire others to dream more, learn more, do more, and become more, you are a leader." By empowering others, leaders transform not only their teams but also themselves, leaving an enduring legacy of trust, innovation, and collaboration.

Chapter 8

MASTERING COMMUNICATION AND INFLUENCE

What really sets leaders apart from managers is what they do. Leaders really know how to see the big picture, motivate people, and get them to think outside the box. On the flip side, managers make things happen by working with others, delegating tasks, tracking results, and ensuring everyone is accountable. When the leaders step onstage, you can see everyone's eyes getting wider. But leaders aren't the ones who control what comes next. Ever met those managers who have everything organized and always keep you on track, but when it comes to actually leading, they struggle to find their way out of a paper bag? One characteristic of both roles is absolutely essential: mastering communication.

The same methods and structures have been employed by skilled communicators throughout history. You will be at risk if you don't understand what they do on a regular basis. To communicate this way, you don't need to be a manager or leader. You will eventually be thrown into one of these roles. All of a sudden, you are in charge because you have the best idea. Your group leader assigns you responsibility for a project, which you must now oversee. Are you prepared to become an expert communicator who knows you can change the world when you get up each morning?

Effective communicators control the reins of power in every office in every country, including presidential elections. They tend to accomplish their goals, their staff enjoy working with them, and their ideas are heard. They observe the communication style of their people. They modify their language to make the point clear to their audience. They know how to listen, and they prepare their words. They have excellent listening skills. The most effective managers and leaders work on the subtleties of their communication skills on a daily basis. Effective communication becomes second nature to them. They genuinely enjoy the times when most people want to flee when they have to deal with the unavoidable flaws in individuals and institutions. They take communication just as seriously as they do money, which makes them the greatest. Too many of us believe that we can communicate improvised, but we don't understand why we don't receive the desired results. We lose a lot of time and money fixing preventable communication errors, whether they happen in front of a large group of people or with clients or coworkers. For the future of their leadership effectiveness and the influence of their teams, master communicators possess the abilities and strategies to establish a communication culture. If people don't value your knowledge, you won't succeed, even if you are the world's most talented professional. In every sector, ideas become reality and concepts become new worlds via deliberate practice and measurement of your message.

Effective communication is a key component of exceptional leadership. Good communication of one's vision, goals, and expectations to the team is the foundation of good leadership. At its core, good communication is more than just exchanging information. It is the capacity to convince people of a vision, settle conflicts calmly, and adapt communications to suit different audiences. Since communication is a two-way street, leaders must also be good listeners. Leaders foster an environment of trust and understanding by listening to their team members.

Persuading, inspiring, and motivating others to take action, make choices, or adopt a particular position is referred to as "communicating with influence." It is the deft application of language, tone, body language, and emotional intelligence to shape and guide other people's beliefs and behaviors. Influential communication does more than just transmit information; it also motivates action and promotes team alignment. Everyone will be working toward the same goal if there is clear and direct communication. Open communication is an essential leadership quality because it encourages a feeling of community and involvement among staff members. Effective communication plans help leaders maximize the potential of their teams and steer them toward success by ensuring alignment, inspiring teamwork, and fostering collaboration.

Needless to say, a leadership development toolkit lacking effective communication might be disastrous. Therefore, in order to lead with impact and inspire their people to do more, leaders must place a high priority on communication, whether it be through written memos, virtual talks, or in-person meetings.

The Art of Clear, Persuasive, And Motivating Communication

Communication is essential to all organizational activities, from everyday operations to strategic planning. The capacity to precisely communicate concepts, establish objectives, and motivate teams is essential for leadership in particular. Clear, convincing, and inspiring communication serves as the cornerstone for flawless execution and harmonious teamwork. Great leaders understand that the foundations of effective communication are motivation, sounding persuasive, and retaining clarity. Team members become confused, misaligned, and disengaged when messages are unclear or confusing. Less productivity will result when communications fail to persuade people to change their opinions or act.

Understanding Clarity in Communication

Clarity in communication means conveying a message that eliminates any possibility of misunderstanding. It guarantees that everyone can understand the expectations, meaning, and aim. Since ambiguity can result in misunderstandings, mistakes, and a decline in trust, this is not only a skill but also a leadership requirement.

Why Leaders Need to Communicate Clearly

1. Minimizes Misunderstandings: By ensuring that everyone is in agreement, mistakes and resources are reduced.

2. Promotes Trust: Openness and trust are fostered by transparent leaders.

3. Increases Productivity: Time is saved and team productivity is increased with clear directions.

4. Strengthens Decision-Making: Well-informed and assured conclusions are the result of precise knowledge.

Ways to Obtain Clarity

Simple Language: Speak in terms that your audience can understand. When using technical phrases, clarify them and steer clear of complicated jargon unless absolutely required.

Concrete Details: To improve comprehension and relatability, support your arguments with particular instances, statistics, or anecdotes.

Logical Structure: Organize data so that it makes sense. For instance, begin with a concise introduction, logically develop the main points, and end with concrete recommendations.

Active Voice: Choose clear, succinct language. As an illustration, "The team accomplished the task" is more understandable than " The task was accomplished by the team."

Audience Awareness: Tailor your message to your audience's interests and degree of understanding. Address technical experts and non-specialists in distinct ways.

Feedback Mechanism: Promote inquiries and confirm comprehension. "Does that make sense?" and "Can I clarify this further?" are examples of phrases that promote two-way communication.

Technical Terms and Jargon: Use them sparingly and give explanation where necessary.

Ambiguous Language: Steer clear of expressions that could be interpreted in several ways. Give specifics.

Overly Complicated Sentences: Divide lengthy sentences into manageable chunks.

Absence of Evidence: To bolster your arguments, back up comments with data or facts.

Developing Clarity

It takes constant practice to become a great leader: Examine previous correspondence and pinpoint areas that require enhancement. Ask mentors or coworkers for their opinions on how well you communicate. Participate in training sessions or workshops on effective communication methods. Effective communication is not just advantageous; it is essential to success. Leaders may inspire confidence, drive results, and create a vibrant organizational culture by embracing these ideas and actively conquering obstacles. Just as important in leadership communication is persuasion. Presenting concepts in a way that is convincing enough to compel belief and action is more important than manipulating others. A compelling leader knows their audience, adjusts their message to fit their values, and provides evidence to support their claims. Any message meant to influence, support, or alter the reactions of another person or people is considered persuasive communication. Such reactions are altered by symbolic transactions (messages) that appeal to the target's emotions and reason and are occasionally, but not always, connected to coercive force (indirectly coercive). Such mediated communicative efforts are generally referred to as persuasion. Face-to-face interactions are referred to as compliance-gaining. The following can be the focus of persuasive communication:

• Cognition. Persuasion can be used to alter people's opinions regarding a variety of topics, such as characteristics, definitions, interpretations, results, etc.

• Mentality. By classifying an object or issue along an evaluative dimension (from bad to good), persuasion can be used to alter people's attitudes regarding such things.
• Conduct. Individuals' overt actions regarding a problem or an object can be changed through persuasion.

Persuasive communication, which blends emotional and intellectual arguments to sway others, is frequently the key to effective leadership. In order to persuade others that a concept or objective is feasible, rational appeals rely on logical arguments and factual data, such as statistics or testimony. The strength of the arguments put forward and the audience's capacity and desire to absorb the material will determine how well they perform. On the other side, emotional appeals use feelings to persuade; classic tactics include guilt and terror. Fear appeals draw attention to dangers and provide doable remedies, highlighting the audience's capacity for successful response as well as the gravity of the threat. Guilt appeals offer a way to ease emotional discomfort by encouraging people to act in a way that is consistent with their values. A leader can more successfully motivate and direct others toward common objectives if they know when and how to use these appeals.

Motivation ties everything together. It is the capacity to arouse others' passion and dedication, frequently by demonstrating sincere concern and comprehending their goals. Because you are in charge, people might follow your instructions, but you might not always get the best output. Most people want to give it their all. Nearly. Despite your best efforts, some followers simply don't give a damn. They act in their own best interests. But a motivating message will go a long way to convince them to act and be committed.

The foundation of successful leadership is a message that is inspiring, convincing, and unambiguous. A leader's communication influences perception and motivates action, whether they are addressing a large group of people, sending an email, or even using non-verbal clues like tone or gestures. Leaders that continuously uphold this standard foster a sense of trust, cooperation, and a common goal among their team members. Great leadership, after all, isn't just about what you say; it's also about how well your message resonates and inspires others to work toward a common objective.

Active Listening and Empathy in Communication

There is a lack of active listening if you are always in a conversation with someone and waiting for them to stop talking so you can say what you want to say or even more, expecting them to pay full attention to what you are saying. This is because you are only considering how you want to respond.

Active listening is essential to making sure that communication is successful because it is a two-way street. All too frequently, leaders concentrate on getting their point across without paying attention to what others have to say. Active listening involves paying attention to tone, body language, and underlying emotions in addition to hearing what is being said. This approach shows respect, fosters trust, and frequently yields insightful information that could otherwise be overlooked.

Empathy and attentive listening are essential components of communication that results in genuine human connection. Making eye contact and acknowledging your attention both verbally and nonverbally are examples of active listening. This includes nodding your head, giving a positive response, and seeking clarification by asking questions.

Active listening and empathy go hand in hand, and empathy is a crucial quality for leaders who wish to forge lasting bonds. Leaders can gain a deeper understanding of their team members' motivations, anxieties, and goals by placing themselves in their shoes. Reflection, affirmation, and a sincere interest in the thoughts and feelings of others are all components of empathy. Empathetic listening, which combines active listening with empathy, can enhance relationships of all types, including those between friends, family, coworkers, and couples.

Everyone wants to feel comfortable expressing their feelings and opinions. It is a vulnerable position to be in when you have the courage to share. If a team member were to discuss a sad, frustrating, or frightening experience with you, consider how they would like you to react. For instance, "I don't get the much needed rest at home, my wife is troublesome." Think about how the person would feel in reaction to these two possible answers:

- Response 1: Oh! I'm happy I'm not you. Care for some coffee?
- Response 2: That must be really difficult. I appreciate you sharing. I am always here for you.

One could feel disregarded by the first response. Why, then, do people react that way? It's possible that the statement originates from the listener's discomfort at hearing anything that appeals to their own vulnerabilities or worries. The listener could feel compelled to end the discussion and find a more secure location. There are moments when people simply aren't sure what to say.

However, one could feel heard, seen, and supported by the second response. This is a result of the second response's empathy. It demonstrates that the listener paid attention to what was being said, expressing compassion (you are not alone) and validating (that must be really difficult).

When someone reveals something challenging with you, how do you know what to say or not say? Sitting and listening is sometimes the best course of action. Empathy is a peculiar and potent force. No script is present. There isn't a proper or improper method to accomplish things. It just involves listening, allowing space, refraining from passing judgment, establishing an emotional connection, and sharing the very reassuring message that "you're not alone.

A lot of us believe we are excellent listeners. However, listening is a talent that requires practice and intention. By being alert throughout discussions, refraining from passing judgment, and posing intelligent, open-ended questions, leaders can develop active listening and empathy. These abilities enable them to establish a more respectful and cooperative atmosphere with their teams and establish a closer connection with them.

Crafting Messages That Resonate with Diverse Audiences

It is crucial to customize your message to meet the unique requirements of each audience while communicating with them. Effective communication with a variety of audiences is an essential business communication skill. Delivering communications that are specific to the requirements and interests of the audience is essential to guaranteeing the project's success. Leaders must adapt their communication to appeal to a wider range of cultures, generations, and backgrounds in the increasingly diverse modern workplace. A one-size-fits-all strategy frequently results in alienation or miscommunication. Good leaders spend time learning about their audience's communication preferences, values, and styles.

Barack Obama, the former president of the United States, was considered a brilliant communicator. His leadership was distinguished by his ability to modify his tone, style, and examples to appeal to a variety of groups, including grassroots organizations and world leaders.

Understanding Your Audience

Knowing the requirements, desires, and interests of your audience is crucial when creating a message. Developing an effective message requires spending time getting to know your audience. You can modify your message to make sure the proper people hear it by knowing who you are speaking to. It's crucial to take into account the audience's aims, values, and prior knowledge of the subject. This can help you think more clearly about how to provide the information in a way that is both pertinent and meaningful. When creating your message, you should also think about the tone and language you utilize. Use language that is appropriate for the audience you are attempting to reach because different audiences may react better to different kinds of language. Lastly, it's critical to take into account the message's delivery medium. For some audiences, different media can be more suitable. For instance, social media might be a better way to reach a wider audience, while email might be more appropriate for talking with coworkers.

Being able to communicate successfully with a variety of audiences is essential for success. Understanding and appreciating communication diversity can improve participation, foster trust, and produce fruitful results in a variety of contexts.

1. Recognizing Cultural Context: People's perceptions and interpretations of communications are influenced by cultural context. Good communicators adapt their messages to appeal to a variety of groups by acknowledging and respecting these cultural variances.

Cultural Awareness will help you learn about your audience's communication preferences, values, and cultural origins.

Also, steer clear of assumptions, and never assume that everyone in a cultural group has the same values or tastes. So, be sensitivity to culture, and be mindful of cultural customs and traditions and refrain from using inappropriate language or imagery.

To do all these properly, ensure cultural competency training, to raise your team's level of cultural understanding, fund training initiatives.

Also, research and put in place a feedback mechanism. To learn about the cultural viewpoints of your target audience, conduct research on them and ask for feedback.

2. Employing Inclusive Language: Inclusive language fosters equity, honors diversity, and communicates respect. It is necessary to establish a setting in which everyone feels appreciated and understood.

Always ensure you use gender-neutral language. To encompass all gender identities, use gender-neutral language (for example, "they" rather than "he/she").

Steer clear of jargon as well. To guarantee accessibility and comprehension for non-native speakers or people who are not familiar with particular terms, use language that is simple and easy to grasp.

Be respectful with the use of terminologies. Steer clear of offensive or out-of-date vocabulary and use phrases that the groups being discussed prefer.

To achieve all of the above, ensure the use of language standards to create and distribute standards for inclusive language in all correspondence. Also keep abreast of changing linguistic inclinations and modify your communication techniques appropriately.

3. Flexible Communication Techniques: It's possible that different audiences will prefer different methods of information delivery. Your message will reach and connect with a variety of audiences if you use adaptive communication techniques.

Audits of accessibility: Make sure your communication materials are in accordance with accessibility standards by conducting routine audits.

Diverse Media: To reach a wider audience, use a variety of media channels and formats.

Adaptive techniques, inclusive language, and cultural understanding are necessary for effective communication with a variety of audiences. Organizations may improve participation, promote inclusivity, and produce favorable results in a variety of circumstances by putting these techniques into practice. In our increasingly globalized society, embracing diversity in communication is not only a recommended practice but also a requirement.

Understanding generational differences and cultural sensitivities improves a leader's capacity to engage their audience. By doing this, they make sure that their vision is accepted as well as understood.

Managing Conflict and Fostering Collaboration

Although conflict is an unavoidable aspect of leadership, a team's success or failure depends on how it is managed. Rather than avoiding confrontation, effective leaders use it as a chance to resolve problems and reinforce bonds with others. The secret to handling conflict is to keep lines of communication open and concentrate on the issue rather than the individual. When a conflict emerges, for example, a competent leader looks for areas of agreement, considers each side's viewpoint, and works together to find a solution. This strategy not only fixes the problem but also upholds a mutually respectful culture.

Clear communication of common objectives and a setting where each team member feels appreciated are essential for promoting teamwork. Collaboration-focused leaders' welcome other points of view, promote brainstorming, and recognize group accomplishments. In addition to raising spirits, this inspires more creative and practical solutions.

Refining Persuasive Communication Skills

By purposeful practice, leaders can improve their communication abilities. The following exercises will help you become more empathetic, persuasive, and clear:

• Situations for Role-Playing: Model difficult discussions, such resolving performance concerns or settling disputes. Consider how well you were able to communicate.

• Storytelling Activities: Get comfortable telling gripping tales that support your goals. Be mindful of the emotional resonance, tone, and structure.

• Feedback Loops: Ask teammates and peers for input on your communication style on a regular basis. Make changes based on their insights.

The Impact of Mastering Communication and Influence

Achieving short-term objectives is only one aspect of mastering influence and communication; another is creating enduring bonds with others and motivating them to give their all. Effective leaders make a lasting impression on their groups and companies. They establish a culture of cooperation, trust, and creativity that lasts long after they go.

The ability to communicate is a dynamic one that develops with experience and practice. You may become the type of leader whose words inspire action and whose influence leaves a legacy by making a commitment to active listening, empathy, and flexibility.

Chapter 9

BALANCING CONFIDENCE AND HUMILITY

H ave you worked with some leaders, and you feel like staying with your leader for a long time? Leaders with courage, good vibes, and strength often have people stay around them for a long time. Every subordinate wants to learn from such a leader. The truth is, one way to know great leaders is how deeply they believe in themselves. This is what we called "Confidence".

"Confidence" is one quality that's frequently used to characterize exceptional leaders. A self-assured leader is a pleasure to work with and follow. A leader's efficacy may be hampered by potential blind spots, though, as is the case with many of our strengths. Arrogance is the blind hole that is frequently connected to confidence. Although followers find confidence in a leader appealing, if it is overdone, it can plant the seeds of mistrust. Followers find it difficult to relate to a leader who exudes confidence. If you are so sure of yourself that you don't contribute, you could come across as unauthentic. The precise balance between humility and confidence is essential for true leadership. While humility keeps leaders grounded, encourages teamwork, and supports personal development, confidence enables them to take calculated risks, inspire trust, and make bold judgments. When these attributes work together, they provide a strong leadership style that is relatable and successful.

Strong Leadership Requires Both Self-Assurance and Humility

Being a leader requires confidence. It is impossible to motivate people, take on obstacles, or make decisions when one lacks confidence. Even during difficult times, teams and stakeholders are reassured by a confident leader's conviction and clarity. Think of leaders like Nelson Mandela, who, in face of overwhelming opposition, inspired millions with his unwavering faith in the potential for a united South Africa.

Confidence on its own, though, might have two drawbacks. Leaders who exhibit overconfidence, characterized by haughtiness or contempt, alienate others and fail to recognize their own faults. Humility acts as a balancing in this situation. Leaders that are humble are able to listen to others, accept their own limitations, and keep learning. It fosters an atmosphere that values many viewpoints, which improves creativity and decision-making.

In essence, a strong leader knows when to trust their own judgment and when to seek input from others. They are able to make decisions while remaining receptive to criticism and cultivate a collaborative environment where team members feel appreciated and empowered to share their ideas. They achieve this by striking a balance between self-assurance (confidence in their abilities) and humility (awareness of their limitations and willingness to learn from others). It takes deliberate work to strike a balance between these two attributes. Without obscuring the efforts and knowledge of others, a leader must exude strength and resolve. They must be able to lead with power while also being personable and receptive to criticism.

Acknowledging Others' Strengths Without Feeling Diminished

Recognizing and applauding others' strengths is one of the characteristics of a humble leader. While confident leaders regard their team members' achievement as a strength, insecure leaders frequently see it as a challenge to their authority. By encouraging others, they fortify the group and show that leadership is about achieving success as a group rather than individual accomplishment.

The former CEO of PepsiCo, Indra Nooyi, is a great illustration of this idea. Nooyi was renowned for her sincere gratitude for the efforts made by her team members, frequently expressing her gratitude in private notes to staff members and their families. In addition to encouraging loyalty, this approach gave others the confidence to assume responsibility for their jobs.

Leaders who practice humility know that acknowledging others does not make them less valuable. Rather, it fosters a climate of mutual respect and trust. They win their teammates' respect and motivate them to reach even higher goals by sharing the limelight.

As a leader, you can employ the following techniques to recognize the strength of others without feeling less than them:

1. Put an end to the competition and comparison. We are aware of the negative effects of comparison and competition, but how can those of us who have been pursuing this destructive habit for years ever quit? It all boils down to altering our internal dialogue—the way we talk to and about ourselves and other people.

    Joy is stolen by comparison. Leaders who compare themselves to others all the time encourage jealousy, insecurity, and resentment. The fact is that comparisons rarely provide a whole picture. You tend to focus on your own shortcomings while ignoring the difficulties of others and focusing on their positives. Insecure competition can create a poisonous atmosphere where cooperation suffers and trust is undermined. Instead, concentrate on teamwork. What can

I contribute to the discussion? How can I continue to believe in my own worth while encouraging others?

Practical Step: Record your accomplishments and other people's contributions every week. Honor both. This easy exercise serves as a reminder that acknowledging the strength of another person does not take away from your own.

2. Accept learning and sharing. Let's alter our perceptions of one another rather than attempting to outdo the next individual. How can we support and benefit from each other? How can we provide support, direction, and assistance? We might be a network of individuals ready to support, encourage, and celebrate one another's accomplishments rather than competing with one another. A leader is never an island. The most successful leaders are aware that they don't have to know everything. They regard the strengths of others as assets rather than threats. In the same way, those around you value your strengths.

Consider leadership as a two-way street in which you both learn and teach. A team culture where everyone feels empowered to contribute without fear of criticism is created by adopting a philosophy of mutual growth.

If a manager has a team member that is exceptionally good at public speaking but struggles with it themselves. The manager could work with that team member to co-present rather than avoiding presentations. The team member feels appreciated for their knowledge, and the manager may eventually become more self-assured.

Realistic Step: Arrange frequent feedback meetings so that team members can exchange ideas. Ask questions, listen intently, and thank them for their efforts.

3. Give Yourself Time to Recover. Being a leader is not without its setbacks and mistakes. Seeing your subordinates thrive where you have failed might be one of the most difficult situations. It's an opportunity to think and develop, but it can also feel humble and even shameful. Give yourself time to think during these times. Being resilient is what it means to be a leader, not being flawless.

Useful Step: Write down your ideas after a failure. Write about your mistakes, your lessons learnt, and your plans for the future. Be kind to yourself and refrain from placing too much blame on yourself or other people.

4. Develop Your self-esteem. Effective leadership is built on a foundation of self-esteem. But it's important to distinguish between arrogance and healthy self-esteem. Having a healthy sense of self-worth enables you to value both yourself and other people.

When you have confidence in yourself, you won't be intimidated by the abilities of others. Rather, you will perceive them as enhancing your own. A leader who found it difficult to delegate because they were afraid of losing control. They will start to trust their team's skills after working on their self-esteem. This change will allow their team members to shine while also reducing their workload.

The goal of leadership is to illuminate the path so that everyone, including yourself, can shine, not to overshadow others. You will develop into the type of leader who fosters respect, cooperation, and trust by eschewing comparisons, embracing learning, giving yourself permission to recover, and boosting your self-esteem.

Allow others' accomplishments to inspire you rather than depress you. Always remember that all boats are lifted by the rising tide.

Approaching Success and Criticism with Balance

Being a leader is a journey with many highs and lows. Leaders' reactions to praise and criticism reveal a lot about their personalities. While humility reminds leaders that their accomplishments are frequently the product of teamwork and outside assistance, confidence allows them to take ownership of their accomplishments without being overly modest.

In a similar vein, when handled with humility, criticism can be a useful instrument for personal development. Leaders who respond defensively to criticism run the risk of offending their teams and passing up chances for development. Conversely, people who see criticism as an opportunity to grow show resiliency and a dedication to improving themselves.

For instance, Amazon founder Jeff Bezos frequently attributed his company's success to his readiness to hear criticism and make necessary adjustments. Amazon was able to keep ahead of the competition and develop constantly because to this mentality.

How to Approach Success

- **Acknowledge Achievements Publicly:** Actively celebrate individual and team accomplishments to ensure everyone feels valued and appreciated.

- **Stay Humble:** Avoid arrogance and overconfidence; remember that success is built on teamwork, and always give credit where it's due.

- **Seek Constructive Feedback:** Regularly ask for input from peers, leaders, and team members to identify growth areas and maintain a mindset of continuous improvement.

- **Invest in Team Growth:** Use achievements as an opportunity to help your team grow by offering new challenges, training, and career development opportunities.

- **Set Fresh Goals:** Keep the team motivated by establishing ambitious new targets and clear visions for the future.

- **Share Knowledge and Insights:** Pass on valuable lessons and ideas to help others grow and succeed within the organization.

- **Adapt to Change:** Stay flexible and ready to adjust plans or strategies to meet the demands of a shifting environment.

- **Lead by Example:** Demonstrate the values and behaviors you want your team to emulate, especially during times of success.

- **Foster a Positive Culture:** Create an environment that celebrates effort and achievement, encouraging a sense of shared success.

How to Approach Criticism

- **Separate the Feedback from the Person:** It's easy to focus on who delivered the critique rather than what they're saying. However, even if you don't fully trust or admire the individual, their message might still hold valuable insights. Aim to evaluate the feedback itself without letting personal feelings about the messenger cloud your judgment.

- **Ask for Specifics:** If the criticism feels unclear or vague, don't hesitate to seek clarification. Asking for concrete examples or elaboration can prevent misunderstandings and help you pinpoint where improvements are needed. Clear communication fosters a better understanding of both your strengths and areas for growth.

- **Manage Emotional Reactions:** Criticism can trigger feelings like defensiveness, frustration, or even hurt. It's natural, but it's important to avoid letting these emotions take over. Pause, take a deep breath, and give yourself time to process before responding. A calm and measured approach is far more productive.

- **Look for the Growth Opportunity:** Every piece of criticism has the potential to teach something valuable. Ask yourself if there's a nugget of truth within it that you can use to grow. Constructive feedback, in particular, is a powerful tool for both personal and professional development.

- **Own Mistakes and Apologize When Necessary:** If the critique is valid, acknowledge it openly and apologize where appropriate. Taking responsibility shows maturity and a willingness to learn, even if you don't entirely agree with every aspect of the feedback.

- **Show Appreciation for Feedback:** Even when feedback is difficult to hear, express gratitude to the person providing it. Thanking them demonstrates that you value the effort they put into offering their perspective. This gesture can also foster mutual respect and trust.

- **Decide on Your Next Steps:** Once you've processed the critique, decide how to proceed. Will you adjust your approach based on the feedback, or stick with your current method after thoughtful consideration? Either way, take action that aligns with your values and goals.

- **Keep Perspective:** Remember that no single piece of criticism defines you or your work. Take the lessons it offers, but don't let it overshadow all your positive attributes or accomplishments. Use the experience as fuel for growth, but remain confident in your overall value and abilities.

By adopting this approach, criticism becomes less of a threat and more of a tool for refining your skills, mindset, and resilience.

How Humility Strengthens Trust and Collaboration

Trust serves as the foundation of effective leadership, and humility is a critical factor in building and sustaining that trust. Leaders who embrace humility are more likely to seek feedback, acknowledge their vulnerabilities, and take responsibility for their mistakes. These behaviors foster authenticity, creating an environment where trust can thrive. When team members observe a leader who values their input and is unafraid to admit imperfections, they feel more confident sharing ideas and taking risks.

Humility also plays a pivotal role in enabling collaboration. Leaders who are genuinely humble cultivate an inclusive atmosphere where diverse perspectives are not only welcomed but deeply valued. By recognizing and appreciating the unique viewpoints of their team, they create a sense of belonging and mutual respect. This inclusive approach not only enhances team cohesion but also leads to better outcomes. Research has shown that teams led by humble leaders tend to be more innovative and productive, as they effectively harness the collective intelligence of their members.

A notable example of humility's impact on leadership and teamwork is Jacinda Ardern, the former Prime Minister of New Zealand. Her empathetic and transparent leadership style earned widespread trust and admiration. Ardern consistently prioritized collaboration and openness, emphasizing shared decision-making and problem-solving. Her approach illustrates how humility can transform leadership into a powerful tool for fostering trust and collaboration, inspiring teams to achieve their best.

Examples Of Leaders Who Exemplify Confidence And Humility

- **Tim Cook, CEO of Apple**

Tim Cook stepped into the monumental role of leading Apple after the iconic Steve Jobs. With quiet confidence, he pursued his vision for the company while embracing collaboration and teamwork. His leadership style prioritizes openness and social responsibility, fostering an environment where innovation thrives. Cook's ability to lead with humility has been instrumental in Apple's continued success, proving that a collaborative approach can sustain greatness.

- **Mother Teresa, Humanitarian Leader**

Mother Teresa's life exemplified servant leadership. Despite her global recognition, she remained deeply humble, focusing on her mission to serve the poor and marginalized. Her modesty and unwavering compassion inspired countless individuals to join her cause, illustrating how humility paired with purpose can create a transformative legacy of kindness and service.

- **Abraham Lincoln, 16th President of the United States**

Abraham Lincoln led the United States through one of its most challenging periods with a blend of confidence and humility. His decision to include diverse perspectives in his cabinet, famously known as the "Team of Rivals," showcased his ability to value differing opinions for the greater good. Lincoln's humility allowed him to prioritize unity and the nation's welfare over personal pride, solidifying his legacy as a thoughtful and inclusive leader.

These leaders demonstrate that true greatness is not just about self-assurance but also about fostering connection, collaboration, and a commitment to serving others. Their examples remind us that humility strengthens leadership and amplifies impact.

Practical Steps to Cultivate Confidence and Humility

Balancing confidence and humility is key to effective leadership. Here are some actionable ways to develop a leadership style that embraces both qualities:

- **Be Open and Receptive**

When making decisions, balance standing by your beliefs with being open to other perspectives. Approach discussions with conviction but also a willingness to learn. For example, instead of rigidly defending your stance, ask questions like, "What am I missing?" or "How does your idea compare?" This mindset shows confidence in your viewpoint while valuing the insights and expertise of others, fostering trust and collaboration.

- **Separate Confidence from Certainty**

True confidence doesn't require knowing all the answers. Leadership often involves making decisions in uncertain situations. Be honest about what you know and the reasoning behind your choices while staying adaptable. For instance, you could say, "Based on the evidence, this seems like the best path forward, but we'll reassess if needed."

This approach reassures your team while promoting flexibility and shared problem-solving.

- **Commit to Lifelong Learning**

Confidence grows through expertise, and humility ensures you stay open to learning. Embrace curiosity and remain teachable, especially in unfamiliar areas. Interact with your team not just as a leader but as someone eager to learn from their experiences and insights. Never let overconfidence prevent you from refining your ideas or exploring new perspectives.

- **Acknowledge Your Limitations**

Recognize areas where you need help, and don't hesitate to ask for support. This openness builds trust and models humility. However, avoid letting humility veer into self-doubt—acknowledging limitations doesn't mean undervaluing your strengths.

- **Celebrate Team Successes**

Shift the spotlight to others whenever possible. Recognize and highlight team members' contributions instead of focusing on your achievements. If you feel the urge to boast, channel it into praising someone else's effort or success. This strengthens team morale and creates a culture of mutual respect.

- **Reflect Regularly**

Take time to evaluate your decisions and actions to ensure they align with your values and leadership goals. Self-reflection helps you recognize areas for growth and adjust your approach as needed.

- **Invite Feedback**

Encourage honest feedback from your team and peers. Be open to constructive criticism and use it as a tool for personal and professional growth. Demonstrating a willingness to improve shows humility and strengthens your connection with others.

By blending confidence with humility, leaders can build trust, foster collaboration, and inspire their teams to reach new heights.

The Legacy of Balancing Confidence and Humility

The true impact of balancing confidence and humility is reflected in the way great leaders inspire and influence those around them. They bring a strong belief in their own abilities but stay genuinely open to learning from others. These leaders understand that humility doesn't take away from their confidence; it makes it stronger. Instead of focusing on how they're perceived, they keep their eyes on the bigger picture, prioritizing their mission over their image.

When leaders achieve this balance, they create environments where innovation and growth flourish. Their ability to build trust and encourage collaboration strengthens teams and drives success. By leading with a focus on serving others rather than serving themselves, they leave behind a legacy of authenticity, empowerment, and integrity.

In practice, this balance means developing qualities that define outstanding leadership. Leaders who seek feedback and welcome questions foster a culture of openness and growth. By recognizing and celebrating the strengths of their team, they build unity and a shared sense of purpose.

Confidence gives them the courage to take risks and make tough decisions, while humility keeps them grounded and open to new ideas. This blend of strength and grace makes their leadership relatable and trustworthy, earning the respect and loyalty of those they guide.

Balancing confidence and humility isn't a one-time achievement—it's an ongoing journey. It takes self-awareness, intentional effort, and a genuine desire to grow. But the rewards are clear: leadership that lifts others, drives meaningful change, and leaves a lasting mark of excellence and service.

Chapter 10

HARNESSING THE POWER OF CRITICAL THINKING

In this chapter, we'll talk about critical thinking; an indispensable skill in a leader's toolbox. In a fast-changing world filled with complex challenges, critical thinking is what sets exceptional leaders apart. It's not just about being knowledgeable or smart; it's about approaching decisions, opportunities, and problems with a clear and logical perspective.

As a leader, you often face situations that aren't black and white. You must weigh competing viewpoints, handle unexpected obstacles, and make decisions that affect not just your team but your organization as a whole. Without critical thinking, it's easy to fall into the trap of snap judgments, following the crowd, or letting emotions drive your choices. But critical thinking pushes you to pause, analyze, and dig deeper to make decisions that are both rational and well-informed.

Why does critical thinking matter? It helps you stay grounded. It enables you to see beyond surface-level problems and uncover their root causes. It also allows you to cut through distractions and focus on what truly matters.

But critical thinking isn't just about solving problems—it's about solving them creatively. It's about finding solutions others might overlook because they didn't question assumptions or ask the right questions.

Our minds, while powerful, are prone to bias, self-interest, and error. Critical thinking acts as a corrective tool, helping us evaluate information objectively. It's a self-aware process where you analyze, synthesize, and assess data from observation, experience, and reflection. This practice is anchored in core principles like fairness, accuracy, and relevance. Skilled critical thinkers naturally guide and refine their thought processes to avoid pitfalls and make sound judgments.

In leadership, the ability to objectively evaluate complex situations is crucial. Without critical thinking, effective leadership is impossible. To lead well and excel in every aspect of intelligent decision-making, leaders must harness this skill. Critical thinking shapes not only how you process information but also how you influence your own behavior and those around you, ultimately defining your success as a leader.

The Importance of Critical Thinking in Leadership

Critical thinking, at its core, is the ability to assess information objectively and analytically to make decisions or solve problems. For leaders, this skill acts like a compass, guiding their choices to be rooted in logic and evidence rather than emotions or assumptions. Without critical thinking, leaders risk making impulsive decisions, falling prey to cognitive biases, or being overly influenced by others' opinions.

The Role of Critical Thinking in Decision-Making

Leaders often face complex situations where straightforward answers are unavailable. In such instances, critical thinking becomes an indispensable tool. By analyzing available information and carefully weighing the pros and cons of each option, leaders can make well-informed choices. This process allows them to avoid hasty decisions and base their actions on reason rather than personal biases or emotional reactions. A leader who relies on critical thinking is better equipped to navigate uncertain or high-stakes situations with confidence and clarity.

Identifying Risks and Opportunities

In today's fast-paced and ever-evolving business environment, the ability to anticipate potential risks and identify opportunities is a key leadership trait. Critical thinking enables leaders to analyze patterns, trends, and data to predict possible outcomes. This foresight helps organizations stay competitive by preparing for potential challenges while capitalizing on emerging opportunities. Leaders who think critically are better positioned to create proactive strategies rather than merely reacting to circumstances as they arise.

Enhanced Communication with Teams

Effective leadership depends on clear and persuasive communication. Critical thinking helps leaders structure their ideas logically, enabling them to present decisions and strategies to their teams in an understandable and convincing manner. This clarity fosters trust and ensures team members fully grasp the rationale behind decisions. Moreover, leaders with strong critical thinking skills are better equipped to address questions or concerns from their teams, leading to greater alignment and commitment to organizational goals.

Encouraging Innovation and Creativity

Innovation is the lifeblood of success in modern businesses. To foster creativity, leaders must challenge conventional ways of thinking and explore new perspectives. Critical thinkers excel in this area by questioning assumptions and seeking out fresh ideas. This mindset allows leaders to devise innovative solutions that might not have been considered otherwise, helping their organizations stay ahead of competitors in a rapidly changing market.

Building Stronger Relationships

Trust and credibility are fundamental to effective leadership. Leaders who engage in critical thinking are better listeners and more empathetic toward their team members' concerns and viewpoints. By demonstrating a willingness to understand different perspectives, leaders can foster a sense of respect and collaboration within their teams. This approach enhances employee engagement and loyalty, both of which are vital for achieving long-term organizational objectives.

Clarity and Focus in Problem-Solving

Miscommunication and confusion often stem from a lack of clarity in understanding or presenting issues. Critical thinkers can distill complex problems into their core elements, making it easier to identify solutions. For instance, a leader addressing a performance decline in their team might avoid jumping to conclusions about laziness or lack of effort. Instead, they would analyze underlying factors, such as burnout, inefficient processes, or unclear objectives, to devise a tailored solution.

By addressing the root causes of problems rather than just the symptoms, leaders save time and resources while instilling confidence in their teams. Employees are more likely to trust leaders who demonstrate thoughtfulness and a commitment to understanding and resolving issues effectively.

The Broader Benefits of Critical Thinking

Critical thinking equips leaders with the ability to gather and evaluate data methodically. By applying logical frameworks and established criteria, they arrive at sound, evidence-based decisions. This approach not only enhances their credibility but also ensures their choices align with organizational values and goals.

Critical thinking is more than just a leadership skill—it is a cornerstone of effective decision-making, innovation, communication, and relationship-building. Leaders who cultivate and apply this ability empower themselves and their teams to navigate challenges with confidence, clarity, and creativity.

Differentiating Between Facts and Assumptions

One of the foundational steps in developing critical thinking is learning to distinguish between facts and assumptions. While this might sound straightforward, the line between the two is not always crystal clear. A fact refers to something that has occurred or is objectively true, often backed by verifiable evidence. On the other hand, an assumption is a belief or idea accepted without proof.

In today's world, the boundaries between assumptions and facts are frequently blurred. As a society, we are often exposed to situations where assumptions are treated as facts. Advertisers, for instance, craft messages designed to influence consumer behavior by presenting assumptions as if they were indisputable truths. Similarly, politicians may leverage assumptions disguised as facts to sway public opinion. Even in personal and professional relationships, assumptions are sometimes used to gain agreement or acceptance, often without supporting evidence.

The Risks of Confusing Assumptions with Facts

While assumptions can sometimes serve as a practical starting point when immediate action is required, relying on them without scrutiny can be risky, particularly for leaders. Decisions made based on unverified or inaccurate assumptions can have far-reaching consequences. Poor decision-making stemming from these errors may lead to decreased trust among team members, misaligned strategies, and setbacks in achieving organizational goals.

For instance, consider a manager observing a dip in team performance. They might assume laziness or lack of commitment is to blame. However, upon closer examination, the real issues could be a lack of adequate resources, unclear expectations, or even burnout among employees. Without distinguishing fact from assumption, the manager might implement ineffective solutions, further exacerbating the problem.

Consequences of Misjudgment

Failing to differentiate between assumptions and facts doesn't just lead to poor decisions—it can create a ripple effect within a team or organization. Confusion and inefficiency often arise when leaders act on assumptions rather than objective evidence. Team members may grow frustrated when decisions seem arbitrary or disconnected from reality. Over time, this can erode morale and undermine the leader's credibility, reducing their ability to inspire and guide effectively.

Strategies to Distinguish Facts from Assumptions

Leaders can refine their decision-making by adopting strategies to discern facts from assumptions. Here are some actionable approaches:

1. **Ask Insightful Questions**

Develop the habit of probing deeper into situations. Questions like *who, what, when, where, why,* and *how* can reveal the underlying details of an issue. By examining core beliefs and challenging initial impressions, leaders can uncover whether their understanding is rooted in fact or conjecture.

2. **Verify Information**

Always cross-check facts using reliable and trustworthy sources. Objective evidence must be separated from subjective opinions to ensure decisions are informed and accurate. Before moving forward, take the time to confirm that what you believe is factual has a solid foundation.

3. **Seek Diverse Perspectives**

Collaborate with team members, peers, or outside experts to gain different viewpoints. Encouraging open, candid discussions can reveal blind spots and reduce the influence of personal biases. By considering multiple perspectives, leaders can form a more well-rounded understanding of the situation.

4. **Test Assumptions**

Before committing to a course of action, consider testing assumptions on a smaller scale. Pilot programs or experiments can provide valuable data and feedback, helping to confirm or challenge initial hypotheses. This approach allows leaders to assess the viability of their assumptions without risking significant resources.

5. **Foster a Culture of Critical Thinking**

Create an environment where critical thinking is encouraged and valued. Allow time for thoughtful analysis rather than rushing into decisions. By promoting a culture that prioritizes evidence-based reasoning, leaders can instill a sense of accountability and thoroughness within their teams.

6. **Document Evidence**

Maintain a record of the information and sources that inform important decisions. By doing so, leaders can ensure transparency and accountability. Additionally, requiring explanations for assumptions encourages a habit of fact-checking and substantiates decisions with verifiable data.

Benefits of Fact-Based Leadership

Leaders who consistently practice differentiating facts from assumptions build stronger trust within their teams. Their decisions carry weight because they are backed by evidence, not guesswork. This approach minimizes risks, improves problem-solving, and leads to more effective and sustainable outcomes. Moreover, it inspires confidence in their leadership, as team members recognize that their decisions are thoughtful, fair, and rooted in reality.

A Balanced Approach

Ultimately, while assumptions may sometimes be necessary for swift action, they should never replace rigorous evaluation and fact-checking. Leaders who take the time to question, analyze, and verify information are better equipped to address challenges, seize opportunities, and drive their teams toward success.

By mastering the ability to differentiate between what is known and what is merely assumed, leaders can create a more informed, balanced, and strategic approach to decision-making. This skill is not just valuable for their personal growth but also essential for building resilient, high-performing teams and achieving organizational goals.

Evaluating Information Objectively and Avoiding Cognitive Biases

Before diving into strategies to overcome cognitive biases, it's essential to understand what they are and how they affect decision-making. Cognitive biases are mental shortcuts and thought patterns that unconsciously influence how we perceive information and make choices. These biases are often shaped by our emotions, personal experiences, cultural background, and societal norms.

On the surface, cognitive biases serve a purpose—they allow our brains to process information quickly and make decisions without being bogged down by analyzing every detail. However, while they save time and effort, these shortcuts often lead to flawed reasoning and poor decisions, especially in situations where stakes are high, or precision is critical.

For leaders, cognitive biases can be particularly detrimental. Unchecked, they can cloud judgment, result in irrational actions, and undermine the ability to make fair and objective decisions. Recognizing and mitigating these biases is a crucial part of leading effectively.

Common Cognitive Biases and How To Avoid Them

1. **CONFIRMATION BIAS**

One of the most prevalent and insidious cognitive biases is confirmation bias. It occurs when individuals seek out or give more weight to information that supports their existing beliefs while ignoring evidence that contradicts them. For example, a leader convinced that a particular strategy will succeed may focus solely on data that reinforces their belief and disregard any opposing evidence.

Combatting confirmation bias requires an active effort to seek out diverse perspectives. Ask yourself, *what is the strongest argument against my belief?* Encourage your team to voice opinions that challenge your assumptions. By fostering an environment where dissenting views are welcomed, you create a safeguard against one-sided thinking.

2. ANCHORING BIAS

Anchoring bias occurs when an initial piece of information disproportionately influences subsequent decisions. For instance, if you are presented with an initial budget estimate that seems reasonable, you might unconsciously use that figure as a baseline, even if later evidence suggests a different amount is more appropriate.

To counter anchoring bias, pause and gather additional information before making a decision. Ask yourself questions like, *Am I holding onto this initial piece of information simply because it was presented first?* Consider alternative data points to ensure that your conclusions are not unduly swayed by the initial anchor.

3. RECENCY BIAS

Recency bias is the tendency to give greater importance to the latest information, even if it isn't the most relevant. This bias often leads to an overemphasis on recent events while neglecting broader patterns or historical data.

Instead of focusing solely on the most recent information, make an effort to examine long-term trends and patterns. Ask questions such as, *Is this data truly representative of the bigger picture?* By balancing recent findings with historical context, you can make more grounded decisions.

4. GROUPTHINK

Groupthink occurs when a team prioritizes harmony and agreement over critical evaluation of ideas. This often happens when individuals feel pressured to conform or fear voicing dissenting opinions. Leaders are especially susceptible to fostering groupthink if they inadvertently suppress disagreement or discourage open dialogue.

Create a safe space where team members feel comfortable sharing differing opinions without fear of judgment. Encourage constructive debate by saying, *I value different viewpoints—what alternatives should we consider?* As a leader, model openness to criticism and reward those who challenge assumptions respectfully.

Why Bias Mitigation Matters For Leaders

Leaders play a pivotal role in shaping organizational decisions and outcomes. When biases go unchecked, they can undermine objectivity, distort judgment, and lead to suboptimal results. This can erode trust within teams, weaken credibility, and harm organizational goals.

By actively recognizing and addressing cognitive biases, leaders can approach problems with greater clarity and make decisions based on facts rather than flawed assumptions. This not only enhances their decision-making but also fosters a culture of critical thinking and accountability within their teams.

Strategies To Promote Objective Thinking

To consistently evaluate information objectively, leaders can adopt the following practices:

1. **Encourage Reflection:** Regularly take time to reflect on your thought processes. Ask yourself, *Am I being influenced by bias, or is my judgment based on evidence?*

2. **Diversify Input:** Surround yourself with people from varied backgrounds and perspectives. A broader range of opinions can help identify blind spots and reduce the risk of bias-driven decisions.

3. **Implement Systems for Feedback:** Create mechanisms that allow team members to provide candid feedback. Constructive input from others can highlight biases you might have overlooked.

4. **Rely on Data and Evidence:** Prioritize data-driven decisions. Whenever possible, use objective metrics to validate assumptions and ensure actions are supported by evidence.

5. **Practice Patience:** Avoid rushing decisions. Taking the time to deliberate and assess all relevant factors helps reduce the influence of snap judgments and biases.

Cognitive biases are an inherent part of human thinking, but they don't have to dominate our decision-making. By understanding their origins and actively working to mitigate their effects, leaders can develop a more balanced, objective approach to evaluating information. This not only improves decision-making outcomes but also inspires confidence among team members, fostering trust and collaboration.

Ultimately, a leader who recognizes and combats cognitive biases demonstrates the kind of critical thinking that is essential for long-term success. With consistent effort, it is possible to transcend these mental shortcuts and lead with clarity, fairness, and integrity.

Developing Problem-Solving Frameworks for Complex Challenges

Leaders are often tasked with navigating complex challenges that cannot be resolved by instinct or guesswork alone. While intuition may play a role, effective leadership requires structured approaches to decision-making. This is where problem-solving frameworks come into play, offering leaders a systematic way to analyze issues, evaluate options, and implement solutions.

Structured problem-solving frameworks help leaders maintain focus, minimize errors, and arrive at decisions that are logical and well-reasoned. By following a clear process, they can address even the most intricate challenges with confidence and precision. One widely recognized and effective framework for tackling complex issues is the **IDEAL model**.

The Ideal Model for Problem-Solving

The IDEAL model is a step-by-step approach designed to break down complex challenges into manageable components. It provides leaders with a roadmap to approach problems logically and systematically, ensuring that all key aspects are considered. Here's a deeper look at each stage of the model:

1. **Identify the Problem**

   The first and most critical step is to clearly define the nature and scope of the problem. Without an accurate understanding of the issue, efforts to resolve it may miss the mark or address only surface-level symptoms.

   Begin by asking questions like:

   o *What exactly is happening?*

   o *What are the contributing factors?*

o   *Who or what is impacted by this problem?*

This step often involves gathering data, consulting with relevant stakeholders, and pinpointing the root cause. For example, if a team is underperforming, the leader might discover that the issue stems from unclear communication rather than a lack of effort.

2. **Define Goals**

Once the problem is clearly identified, the next step is to outline what success looks like. Establishing clear goals provides direction and a benchmark against which progress can be measured.

Effective goal-setting involves defining outcomes that are:

o   **Specific**: Clearly articulate the desired result.

o   **Measurable**: Ensure progress can be tracked quantitatively or qualitatively.

o   **Achievable**: Set realistic expectations based on available resources.

o   **Time-bound**: Establish a timeline for achieving the objectives.

For instance, if the problem involves customer dissatisfaction, the goal might be to improve satisfaction scores by 20% within six months through enhanced service delivery.

3. Examine Alternatives

With the problem identified and goals defined, the next step is to brainstorm and evaluate possible solutions. Consider all viable options, even those that may initially seem unconventional.

During this phase, it's helpful to:

o Weigh the **pros and cons** of each option.

o Assess the feasibility of implementation.

o Anticipate potential risks and challenges associated with each choice.

Collaborating with team members or subject-matter experts can provide valuable insights and foster creative thinking. Remember, the best solution is often not the most obvious one but the one that aligns most closely with the established goals.

4. Execute the Plan

Once a course of action is selected, it's time to put the plan into motion. Execution is where strategy meets reality, and it requires careful coordination and communication.

Effective execution involves:

o Delegating tasks clearly to ensure accountability.

o Monitoring progress regularly to identify and address obstacles.

o Remaining adaptable to make adjustments as new information arises.

For example, if the chosen solution involves rolling out a new process, leaders should ensure proper training for team members and establish checkpoints to measure effectiveness.

5. **Reflect and Learn**

After the solution has been implemented, it's essential to evaluate the outcome. This step is often overlooked but is vital for continuous improvement. Reflection allows leaders to understand what worked, what didn't, and how similar challenges can be addressed more effectively in the future.

Key questions to consider during this phase include:

o *Did the solution achieve the desired goals?*

o *What were the unexpected challenges, and how were they handled?*

o *What lessons can be applied to future problem-solving efforts?*

Documenting these insights not only enhances the leader's personal growth but also builds organizational knowledge that can benefit the team or company in the long run.

Benefits Of Using a Structured Framework

By adopting a structured problem-solving framework like the IDEAL model, leaders can approach challenges with greater clarity and confidence. This methodical approach minimizes the risk of oversight, ensures consistency in decision-making, and fosters a culture of accountability and learning.

In addition, structured frameworks encourage collaboration, as they provide a common language and process for tackling problems. Team members are more likely to engage and contribute when they understand the steps being taken and their role in the process.

Complex challenges are an inevitable part of leadership, but they don't have to be overwhelming. With a structured framework like the IDEAL model, leaders can break down even the most daunting problems into manageable steps. By identifying the issue, setting clear goals, evaluating alternatives, implementing solutions, and reflecting on outcomes, they can not only address immediate challenges but also build their capacity for future success.

In a world of constant change and uncertainty, the ability to approach problems systematically is an invaluable skill. Leaders who master this approach are better equipped to lead their teams with confidence, achieve their objectives, and drive meaningful progress.

Practicing Critical Thinking

Critical thinking is a cornerstone of effective leadership, enabling leaders to approach challenges with clarity, logic, and informed decision-making. While some individuals may have a natural aptitude for it, critical thinking is a skill that can be cultivated through deliberate practice and consistent effort. Leaders can enhance their critical thinking abilities by engaging in activities that challenge assumptions, promote self-reflection, and sharpen problem-solving skills.

Practical Ways to Practice Critical Thinking

1. **Case Analysis**

Analyzing real-world scenarios where difficult leadership decisions had to be made is an excellent way to practice critical thinking. By examining the outcomes and considering alternative strategies, leaders can gain valuable insights into decision-making processes. This exercise not only enhances problem-solving skills but also provides a broader understanding of potential outcomes.

2. **Reflective Journaling**

Writing down decisions, thoughts, and lessons learned in a journal can be a powerful tool for self-reflection. Regularly reviewing these entries allows leaders to identify patterns in their thinking, recognize biases, and pinpoint areas for improvement. Over time, this practice helps in cultivating a mindset of continuous learning.

3. **Group Discussions**

Engaging in group debates or discussions on controversial topics can help leaders develop their ability to articulate and defend their viewpoints. These exercises encourage rational argumentation, active listening, and openness to alternative perspectives, all of which are essential components of critical thinking.

4. **Role-Playing Exercises**

Simulating real-world leadership challenges, such as managing a crisis or resolving team conflicts, allows leaders to test their decision-making skills under pressure. These exercises foster adaptability and help leaders evaluate their ability to analyze situations critically and respond effectively.

The Broader Impact of Critical Thinking

Critical thinking does not just influence personal decision-making; it shapes the culture of an organization. Leaders who consistently demonstrate analytical thinking set an example for their teams, encouraging them to approach problems thoughtfully and embrace a mindset of continuous improvement.

Organizations led by critical thinkers tend to be more innovative, resilient, and adaptive. Such environments thrive in uncertainty because their leaders prioritize well-informed decisions and careful deliberation, fostering a culture where challenges are seen as opportunities for growth.

Developing Critical Thinking Skills

Improving critical thinking is an ongoing journey, and focusing on foundational skills is a great way to begin. Here are some critical areas to prioritize:

1. **Inference**

Inference involves drawing logical conclusions from incomplete or ambiguous information. Leaders skilled in inference are less likely to jump to conclusions and more likely to explore all available evidence before making decisions.

2. **Bias Recognition**

Recognizing and addressing biases is vital for objective decision-making. Biases can distort perceptions and lead to flawed conclusions. Leaders should strive to gather reliable evidence and critically evaluate information sources to minimize bias.

3. **Establishing Relevance**

Not all information is equally important. Leaders must identify the most pertinent details and avoid distractions that may carry a hidden agenda. This skill ensures that decisions are based on meaningful and actionable insights.

4. **Evaluating Arguments**

Arguments often aim to persuade and may be influenced by inherent biases. Leaders can counteract this by researching independent sources and basing their evaluations on objective evidence.

Actionable Strategies for Improvement

1. **Commit to Lifelong Learning**

o **Read Widely**: Dive into books, articles, and research papers covering topics like leadership, psychology, and industry trends. Exposure to diverse perspectives fuels creativity and problem-solving.

o **Attend Workshops**: Enroll in seminars or professional development courses that introduce new ideas and challenge existing beliefs.

o **Stay Updated**: Keep abreast of economic, technological, and industry changes through networking, conferences, and reputable newsletters.

2. **Seek Mentorship**

o **Find Experienced Leaders**: Work with mentors known for sound judgment and analytical thinking.

o **Learn Actively**: Observe how they navigate challenges, ask thoughtful questions about their decision-making processes, and apply those lessons to your leadership style.

o **Request Feedback**: Share your experiences and solicit constructive criticism to refine your approach to problem-solving.

3. **Foster a Team Culture of Critical Thinking**

o **Encourage Open Dialogue**: Create an environment where team members feel safe to voice opinions and challenge assumptions. Diverse perspectives lead to well-rounded solutions.

o **Provide Training**: Offer resources and workshops focused on analytical thinking, problem-solving, and decision-making skills.

o **Celebrate Innovation**: Recognize and reward creative ideas and thoughtful contributions, reinforcing the value of intellectual curiosity.

4. **Cultivate Self-Awareness**

o **Evaluate Personal Biases**: Regularly reflect on your own assumptions and beliefs to minimize their impact on your decisions.

- o **Practice Mindfulness**: Techniques like journaling or meditation can enhance focus and clarify thought patterns.

- o **Welcome Honest Feedback**: Ask trusted colleagues or mentors to point out blind spots in your thinking, and use their insights to improve.

The Lasting Value of Critical Thinking

Critical thinking is more than just a skill—it's a mindset that equips leaders to navigate complexity with integrity and confidence. Leaders who practice critical thinking inspire their teams to think more deeply, innovate more boldly, and approach challenges with a thoughtful perspective.

This mindset is not innate but develops through consistent practice. By incorporating critical thinking into daily routines, leaders can enhance their ability to tackle challenges effectively while leaving a legacy of sound decision-making that positively impacts both individuals and organizations.

In a fast-changing world, critical thinking is not just an advantage—it is essential for sustained success and meaningful leadership

CONCLUSION

Leadership is not a destination; it's a journey. It requires an all-time commitment to personal and professional development, readiness to change, and the modesty to learn from both successes and failures. The dimensions of leadership that have been explored in this book range from vision building, mastering communication, balancing confidence with humility, and using critical thinking. I would now like to turn to the big picture: how leaders develop over time and sustain their momentum.

Great leaders come to understand that growth cannot end with accomplishment but is rather something to be continued. Lifelong learning is more than an acquisition of knowledge; it's the enrichment of self-awareness, including expanded perspectives and adaptability, which will help move along with life in constant flux.

Self-Reflection: Take a step back to reflect on your leadership style, decisions, and impact. What lessons have shaped you? Which areas need further development?

Surround yourself with people who challenge and support you. Constructive feedback is a major way to see areas of improvement.

Pursue knowledge: Read books or attend seminars or professional development programs. The acquisition of knowledge will keep you relevant and resilient.

For example, Nelson Mandela's life was a good example of lifelong learning: after spending 27 years in prison, he came out with greater understanding of leadership, forgiveness, and diplomacy, which he then used to unify his divided nation.

Leadership is not something that one obtains or attains; it's only a dynamic, moving experience. Major milestones in this journey celebrate growth, setbacks test one's resiliency, and triumphs reassure purpose. At its core, leadership isn't really about imperfection; it's more so about embracing the process of growing and moving forward.

Continual reflection on experiences, learning from failures, and celebrating small victories are all indicative of development as a leader. Each challenge holds an opportunity to sharpen decision-making skills, improve communication, and strengthen relationships. It is not about finally having the right answers; it is about having the humility to ask the right questions, listen to diverse perspectives, and adapt.

Furthermore, true leadership is not a reflection of selfishness; it stands out with regard to how well it inspires others to create a space for growth, contribution, and success. A developing leader understands that his/her work is not only to lead from the front but to encourage others, shine together, work in harmony, and achieve common objectives.

And in this journey, detours are not failure; they become stepping stones toward future success. Errors become lessons; challenges build character. A wonderful leader is never afraid of imperfections; rather, he revels in them as an important ingredient for arriving at his best self and, with that, leading others to do the same.

Leadership evolution is about progress, not perfection—a commitment to grow and improve through every phase of the journey.

A real leader is not measured by title, prestige, or recognition but by the lives he or she has touched and the footprints he or she has left behind. Leadership is about having a positive ripple effect in all directions—a positive ripple effect that goes far beyond your immediate sphere of influence.

Whether it's a multinational, a small team, or even a family you're leading, your journey counts. It speaks to strength in vision, tenacity, and integrity—the very stuff that makes home.

As I draw the conclusion of this book, think about your own journey as a leader. How will you grow, adapt, and inspire? The evolution of a leader is never really done; it is a lifelong commitment to making a difference one decision, one relationship, and one moment at a time.

REFERENCES

- Edmondson, A. (1999). *"Psychological Safety and Learning Behavior in Work Teams."* Administrative Science Quarterly.

- Brown, T. (2009). *Change by Design: How Design Thinking Creates New Alternatives for Business and Society.*

- Amabile, T. M. (1998). "How to Kill Creativity." Harvard Business Review.*

- Johnson, S. (2010). *"Where Good Ideas Come From: The Natural History of Innovation."*

- *Harvard Business Review* (2020). "The Neuroscience of Trust."

- Findings on the importance of trust in leadership as a driver of workplace satisfaction.   Source: *PwC's 2016 Global CEO Survey.*

- Business Insider and Microsoft Leadership Case Studies. Source: *BBC News* and *The Guardian*

- Buckingham, M., & Clifton, D. O. (2001). *Now, discover your strengths.* Free Press.

- Covey, S. R. (1989). *The 7 habits of highly effective people: powerful lessons in personal change.* Free Press.

- Parsloe, E. & Leedham, M. (2009). *Coaching and mentoring: Practical techniques for developing learning and performance.* Kogan Page.

- Sinek, S. (2014). *Leaders eat last: Why some teams pull together and others don't.* Portfolio/Penguin.

- Mandela, N. (1994). *Long walk to freedom: The autobiography of Nelson Mandela.* Little, Brown, and Company.

- Branson, R. (2014). *The Virgin way: If it's not fun, it's not worth doing.* Portfolio.

- Gates, B. (2007). *Remarks at Harvard University commencement.* Retrieved from www.gatesfoundation.org

- Wooden, J. (2003). *Wooden on leadership: How to create a winning organization.* McGraw Hill.

- Angelou, M. (2008). *Letter to my daughter.* Random House.

- Doran, G. T. (1981). *There's a S.M.A.R.T. way to write management goals and objectives. Management Review, 70*(11), 35–36.

- Spreitzer, G. M. (1995). *Psychological empowerment in the workplace: Dimensions, measurement, and validation. Academy of Management Journal, 38* (5), 1442–1465.

- Seligman, M. E. P. (2011). *Flourish: A Visionary New Understanding of Happiness and Well-being.* Free Press.

- Duckworth, A. (2016). *Grit: The Power of Passion and Perseverance.* Scribner.

- Bowley, G. (2011, September 10). *Cantor's Grieving Chief Endures, With A Nod to 9/11 Families.* The New York Times. Retrieved from https://www.nytimes.com

- Belvedere, M. J. (2021, September 11). *Cantor Fitzgerald CEO Howard Lutnick reflects on 9/11 tragedy and recovery.* CNBC. Retrieved from https://www.cnbc. com

- "Jamie Dimon on the Financial Crisis: A Decade Later." *Harvard Business Review*, October 2018. Retrieved from https://hbr.org.

-

- Rieker, M. (2009, January 27). *How JPMorgan Chase weathered the financial crisis*. The Wall Street Journal. Retrieved from https://www.wsj.com

- McGregor, J. (2020, April 8). *Marriott CEO Sorenson's powerful message to furloughed workers*. The Washington Post. Retrieved from https://www.washingtonpost.com

- Harreld, H. (2020, March 20). How Marriott's CEO addressed employees amid COVID-19. Forbes. Retrieved from [https://www.forbes.com

- Goleman, D. (2013). *Focus: The Hidden Driver of Excellence*. HarperCollins.

- Collins, J. (2001). *Good to Great: Why Some Companies Make the Leap...and Others Don't*. HarperCollins.

- Dweck, C. S. (2006). *Mindset: The New Psychology of Success*. Random House

- Goleman, D. (1995). *Emotional Intelligence: Why It Can Matter More Than IQ*. Bantam Books.

- Boyatzis, R. E., & McKee, A. (2005). *Resonant Leadership: Renewing Yourself and Connecting with Others Through Mindfulness, Hope, and Compassion*. Harvard Business School Press.

- Druskat, V. U., & Wolff, S. B. (2001). "Building the Emotional Intelligence of Groups." *Harvard Business Review*, 79(3), 80-90.

- McKee, A. (2018). *How to Be Happy at Work: The Power of Purpose, Hope, and Friendship*. Harvard Business Review Press.

- Brownell, J. (2012). *Listening: Attitudes, Principles, and Skills*. Pearson.

- Galinsky, A. D., et al. (2008). "Perspective-taking: Debunking the Myths, Discovering the Value." *Journal of Applied Psychology,* 93(5), 895–909.

- Schilling, M. A. (2009). *Strategic Management of Technological Innovation.* McGraw-Hill Education.

- Dweck, C. S. (2006). *Mindset: The New Psychology of Success.* Random House.

- Ashford, S. J., & Cummings, L. L. (1983). "Feedback as an Individual Resource: Personal Strategies of Creating Information." *Academy of Management Journal, 26(3), 465-486.*

- Catmull, E., & Wallace, A. (2014). *Creativity, Inc.: Overcoming the Unseen Forces That Stand in the Way of True Inspiration.* Random House.

- Garvin, D. A. (2013). "How Google Sold Its Engineers on Management." *Harvard Business Review.*

- Carmeli, A. (2003). "The Relationship Between Emotional Intelligence and Work Attitudes, Behavior, and Outcomes." *Journal of Managerial Psychology*, 18(8), 788–813.

- Gallup (2020). *The State of the American Workplace Report.*

- Businessolve. (2019). *The State of Workplace Empathy.* Annual survey examining the role of empathy in employee retention and engagement.

- Ignatius, A. (2015). "The CEO of Microsoft on Rediscovering the Company's Soul." *Harvard Business Review.*

Made in the USA
Thornton, CO
01/10/25 21:18:48

1c215937-6787-487b-ad81-d040a3b97fa8R01